When the Horizons Close

Rereading Ecclesiastes

ELSA TAMEZ

Translated from Spanish by Margaret Wilde

ORBIS BOOKS
Maryknoll, New York 10545

The Catholic Foreign Mission Society of America (Maryknoll) recruits and trains people for overseas missionary service. Through Orbis Books, Maryknoll aims to foster the international dialogue that is essential to mission. The books published, however, reflect the opinions of their authors and are not meant to represent the official position of the society.

To obtain more information about Maryknoll and Orbis Books, please visit our website at www.maryknoll.org.

Library of Congress Cataloging-in-Publication Data

Tamez, Elsa
    [Cuando los horizontes se cierran. English]
    When the horizons close : rereading Ecclesiastes / Elsa Tamez ; translated from Spanish by Margaret Wilde.
      p. cm.
    Includes bibliographical references.
    ISBN 1-57075-313-x (paper)
    1. Bible. O.T. Ecclesiastes—Commentaries. I. Title.

BS1475.3.T36 2000
223'.8077—dc21

                    99-058009

CONTENTS

PREFACE

The Book of Qoheleth or Ecclesiastes has become timely again today, when horizons are closing in and the present becomes a hard master, demanding sacrifices and suppressing dreams.

Today, at the beginning of the millennium, we are experiencing at the global level a lack of hope that there will be good times for all in the near future. We feel impotent when confronted with the dehumanizing reality caused by unemployment, profound social differences, discriminations of all kinds, and the growing callousness and lack of solidarity. All of this is the result of the so-called nonintentional effects of the free market. To this is added the lack of alternatives that could give light to a possible practice that would enable us to move forward. Anguish reigns, the spirit is crushed, life is diminished and paralyzed. All of us, in some way, for different reasons, have felt this sensation of closed horizons. For this situation, even though it seems incredible, the book of Ecclesiastes has something to say.

By reading Qoheleth in both today's context and its own context, we can see it from angles that we hadn't seen before: fresh perspectives that affirm real, everyday life with its feelings and sensuality; spaces of good life and grace in the midst of a dehumanizing present, and in the face of inscrutable horizons. We see Qoheleth's wise sayings as rays of light, shining through the cracks in a dark, depressing room. They enlighten without hiding the total frustration that people felt under the sun in his own time. They are the advice of a sage in the third century B.C.E. who is living in the province of Palestine during the "globalization" of the Hellenistic Ptolemaic system based in Alexandria, the center of the Greek-Macedonian empire in Egypt. "There is nothing new under the sun," he writes to the aristocrats of his day, who are oppressed and dazzled by the new technology, and by the efficiency of the Greek production, commerce, and culture coming out of the imperial metropolis. This little book is dedicated to the reader. More than a classical commentary, it is a proposed way of reading the scripture for our hopeless times. I want to explore his utopian reasoning in the midst of his frustration—a frustration that never quite disappears from his discourse, which opens and closes with the disconcerting words: "Vanity of vanities, says the Teacher; all is vanity" (1:2; 12:8).

I have divided the book into three parts or sections,[1] plus an introduction. At the beginning of each part there is a commentary on the whole section. Similarly, in analyzing each unit within the sections I offer a synthesis before going into the details of each verse. Readers may find that this method leads to repetition. At the end there is an appendix of sayings or proverbs that reflect the complexity of life and the popular wisdom needed to endure the times of frustration under the sun. The overall framework for my proposal is found in the introduction, "Taking It All Together."[2]

INTRODUCTION

Qoheleth: Taking It All Together

An insistent concern with the theme of hope, now at the end of the millennium, reveals a crisis of hope and a need to rebuild utopia in our own time.

The present despair is the result of systematic pressure from the ideology of capitalism, according to Franz Hinkelammert. The strategy is to create "a culture of despair." Indeed, to have hope in a different kind of future threatens the stability of the present global economic system, whose supporters believe that simply applying it will lead directly to a perfect society.[1] That system is supposed to mean hope for all, and to create other hopes is to work against the only viable hope. Therefore one must not have other expectations, but rather live in the promised hope and readjust it as necessary. If that is so, then for those who are looking for new realities of life for everyone, reflecting on utopia becomes an urgent priority.

A reason for living, or the meaning of life, is one of the most profound and universal questions that human beings have asked through the centuries. It entails an effort, often in vain, to understand future events in history and even beyond earthly existence. To seek the reason for living is not just a philosophical concern; it comes from our desire to live with dignity in the face of conflicts and challenges, whether these are economic, cultural, social, or political.

It would seem that when the future becomes so terribly inscrutable, utopia hides itself; it is nowhere to be found. When utopia cannot be created, human fulfillment is also impossible.

1

And when human fulfillment is impossible, so is the society we seek to create.

The book called Eccesiastes, or Qoheleth, written around the second half of the third century B.C.E.,[2] during the Ptolemaic empire, raises this problem. The narrator experiences reality as a great emptiness, masked by the change and agitation around him; he is anguished by his inability to envision a liberating future; and amid this crisis of meaning he reflects on the inevitability of death and the impossibility of effectively challenging God's intentions. He exhorts the people at that crossroad to enjoy the happy moments of the present: to eat and drink and find enjoyment in their toil. This approach to history is an anomaly in the biblical history of salvation, which usually overflows with messianic promises and hopes. What is the meaning of Qoheleth's unusual way of confronting uncertainty? Can this proposal be valid for our time? How should we interpret his approach and the reasons for it? These are some of the questions we shall ask, in analyzing the book of Qoheleth.

In this study we shall approach the problem of utopia from the experience of the wise Qoheleth. We shall reflect on his perception of reality, his implicitly utopian horizon, the enigma of God, the influence of the times, and the possible alternatives he offers along the way. Perhaps we shall find in this canonical book some critical word to give us a better understanding of certain modern-day situations and attitudes that occur when horizons are closing. It would seem that this is the only book of the Bible that "abandons the biblical vision of history understood as a divine project in progressive linear, 'messianic' development."[3]

THE WORLD NARRATED BY QOHELETH: THERE IS NOTHING NEW UNDER THE SUN

Everything Is *Hebel*

Qoheleth's perception of the world is framed by the words that appear at the beginning and the end of this literary work:[4]

"Vanity of vanities, says the Teacher, vanity of vanities! All is vanity."

Between the beginning and the end, the narrator conducts an internal debate through monologues, intense at times, trying to find meaning in a meaningless life.

He begins by sketching his perception symbolically, with a poem that can make the reader dizzy with its rapid and monotonous circularity (1:4-11).

The cyclical turns of the sun, the wind, and the rivers not only describe the absence of anything new or unforeseen; the key words affect the reader's body, producing something like seasickness and nausea from the incessant ups and downs. Qoheleth's malaise comes from his perception of the world, and he makes his readers feel it too. He describes it with the Hebrew word *hebel*. All of reality as he lives, observes, and reflects on it is described as *hebel*. Our versions of the Bible translate this as "vanity," but that word does not fully convey what Qoheleth is trying to say. In modern slang perhaps, less abstract words than vanity or absurdity—such as "worthless," or "rubbish," or "shit"—would better express his frustration with what goes on under the sun.[5]

We might read the repetitive superlative in 1:2 as follows: "A big mess, says the Teacher, a big mess! Everything is messed up." Gianfranco Ravasi prefers to translate the Hebrew superlative as "an immense emptiness."[6] In a way, that feeling—like "an emptiness in the stomach"—is what comes when reality is perceived as a mess, when apparently there is no way to change the course of history and there are no visible signs that human fulfillment is possible.

The Conspiracy of the Times

Qoheleth's view of time is the key to a reading that allows us to breathe with a certain serenity and makes life more bearable, less anguishing, in the midst of the immense emptiness or the "great *hebel*." In order to discern that there is a time and a season for everything, he must struggle against the present, the future, and the past; these three seem to conspire against any structural possibility for a dignified life, a life worth living, for everyone. Neither in the present, nor in the future, nor in the past does Qoheleth find a handle to grasp as he tries to envision an attractive utopia and place his faith in it. There is nothing new under the sun.

The present is *hebel*, vain; it is like the frustration of someone who cracks open a luscious nut and finds it dried up. The future offers nothing new, nothing to struggle for, no hope of victory; it is all fruitless. As if the nutshell were transparent and one could see that there was nothing inside. The future is strangled by the affirmation that everything that will happen has already happened, and that every event will be forgotten. Neither the liberating history of the God of the exodus nor the messianic visions of Second Isaiah—delivered at the return from exile in Babylonia—come into Qoheleth's view; they have all evaporated. Besides, he is convinced that no one can know the future.

There is no memory of the past. The marvelous acts of God the liberator from slavery in Egypt, told and remembered from generation to generation, have also fallen into oblivion. No one remembers the taste of a good nut. There is no separation of times, nor any discord among them. It is as if history were suspended, or "in a comatose state," while Palestine passed from the hand of the Babylonian empire to the Persian empire, and now to the Hellenistic Ptolemaic empire. All the questions demand a negative answer (1:9-11).

The horizons are closed. No matter how he tries, Qoheleth cannot know the future or see any good for humanity beyond the future; all he can do is keep asking questions (6:12; 8:7).

The Experience of *Hebel* in Everyday Life

Let us now see what happens in daily life under the sun, which in Qoheleth's eyes is *hebel*, "emptiness," "absurd," or worthless.

"Enslaving" Toil

At the beginning of his discourse the narrator complains about enslaving labor. He describes it with the Hebrew term *ʿamal.*[7] The word came late into the Hebrew vocabulary, because wearying labor was experienced only with the advent of agriculture; one must also remember that that was when slavery began to play an important part in the production methods of the time. What Qoheleth sees as absurd, *hebel,* is that people work laboriously without reaping the benefit of their labor or being able to enjoy it. He repeatedly questions the advantages of work. This is one of the key questions that help us understand why Qoheleth is weary of his world and sees no possible way out except to eat and drink with serenity and joy in the midst of enslaving toil. As we have said before, his writing begins in v. 2 with a superlative affirmation about the reality of *hebel* and continues with the question that pierces his conscience: "What do people gain from all the toil (*ʿamal*) at which they toil under the sun?" (1:3; 2:22; 3:9).

Speaking negatively of wearisome, fruitless toil, Qoheleth makes an example of himself as a figurative king. He has done many material things: he became wise; he enjoyed whatever he could. Qoheleth, taking on that character, comes to criticize his own rulers or the powerful ones of his time, because everything they did was vanity (*hebel*) and a chasing after wind (1:14).[8]

Unlike many others, this character was able to draw some enjoyment from his work; he says this was his reward for all his toil (2:10). But even so, all his hard work falls into the category of *hebel* because others take control of what he has produced. That is why Qoheleth's spirit is so enraged that he abhors life and his own work; we see his rage in 2:17, 21.

The narrator-protagonist gives several reasons why there is no benefit from the product of toil. One of these is labor so enslaving that it turns life into pain and work into a vexation and does not allow rest even at night (2:23).

Another is that the product of his work is taken from him, as we saw above, or because human beings are dominated by the desire to accumulate wealth. Some people work tirelessly and do not even have a loved one with whom to share the fruits of their work (4:8). Qoheleth criticizes the love of money. Those who love it never get their fill, and there is no benefit in having much. Why? Because when goods increase the consumers also increase, and then the owner only sees his gain with his eyes (5:11); also because abundance does not let him sleep sweetly as the simple laborer does (5:12).

Accumulated wealth brings only ill to the owners: it may be lost in a bad venture, and there is nothing left for the owner's children (5:14). Finally, when the owners die they go away naked, with nothing in their hands but darkness, vexation, sickness, and resentment (5:17).

Thus, for Qoheleth, not enjoying the fruit of labor is what turns the whole process of labor and life in general into *hebel*. Even those blessed by long life (two thousand years) and many children (a hundred),[9] if they are not able to enjoy even a day of happiness, and if they have no one to bury them, gain nothing from being born. In this sense a stillborn child is better off than they. That child at least does not see what is happening under the sun (6:2-6).

Even work itself, well done, does not escape Qoheleth's critical eye: he sees no possibility of human fulfillment in the work process. But he cannot abandon it, because work is necessary for survival. In 4:4-5 he says that all toil and all skill awaken the envy of others against their neighbor. "This also is 'an absurdity' and a chasing after wind," and as for those who do not work: "Fools fold their hands and consume their own flesh" (4:5). Thus it is better to have "a handful with quiet than two handfuls with toil and a chasing after wind" (4:6).

Injustice as the Order of the Day in an Inverted World

At several points Qoheleth alludes to oppression and injustice. He talks about the perversion of values. He sees that wickedness and justice have changed places (3:16; 4:1). One perceives in his world a very repressive situation and a great lack of solidarity. The greatest frustration is that what one hopes for never arrives. One hopes for justice in the courts and finds the opposite. The same is true of the wisdom and prophetic traditions, which affirm that all goes well with the righteous, while the unrighteous suffer evil and their days are shortened. The retributive schema of the wisdom tradition comes into crisis when faced with concrete experience. The schema is not historically verified, for what Qoheleth sees under the sun is very different, quite the opposite: "In my life of *hebel* I have seen everything; there are righteous people who perish in their righteousness, and there are wicked people who prolong their life in their evildoing" (7:15). Later he repeats the same affirmation (8:14).

The horizons are closing in because, for our narrator, the least that he hopes for never comes. The inversion of values does not allow him to hypothesize any possibility of justice. And where there would be some likelihood of judgment for evil, it does not happen. Because the sentences are not carried out, there is no reason to hope for anything new under the sun. Impunity aggravates criminality (8:11). The state institutions set up for the right ordering of society are entangled in a bureaucratic complicity that discourages any belief in the possibility of claiming a right: "If you see in a province the oppression of the poor and the violation of justice and right, do not be amazed at the matter; for the high official is watched by a higher, and there are yet higher ones over them" (5:8).[10]

Taking Power Does Not Guarantee the Desired Outcome

Apparently this political practice does not work in Qoheleth's world either, as he explains with a small story buried in the text (4:13-16). There is a poor but wise youth, and there is an old but foolish king. This reality contradicts the tradition that the grey hairs of the old make them wise and that youth lack the wisdom of the old because they have so much to learn. Moreover, kings are descended from rich and noble families. Curiously, Qoheleth turns this normal state of things around. He prefers the poor but wise youth to the old king who will not take advice. The youth was in prison, and he came out as a ruler, with the total support of the people: "I saw all the living who, moving about under the sun, follow that youth who replaced the king; there was no end to all those people whom he led" (4:15-16a).

But Qoheleth foresees the end of this new possibility before it comes and announces its future failure: "Yet those who come later will not rejoice in him. Surely this also is *hebel* and a chasing after wind" (4:16bc).

Why does the writer make the narrator so distrustful of a change of power? Perhaps in its context, this is what his people have experienced in the changes of empire and the empty hopes of his contemporaries for a better life—from Sennacherib to Nebuchadnezzar, from Nebuchadnezzar to Alexander the Great, and then to the Ptolemies and the Seleucids, and later the Romans. Or perhaps he was referring to the wars between the Ptolemies and the Seleucids over the control of Palestine, which recurred several times in the hundred years of Ptolemaic rule from Egypt after the death of Alexander. Qoheleth's contemporaries kept harboring illusions about one or another of these. Another possibility is that he was saying that all exercise of power is doomed to failure. In either case, for him political power offers no possible horizons for change to a more egalitarian society. Before that possibility even appears, he announces its unfortunate end.

The Need to Walk Cautiously in Economics and Politics

In several parts of the text the narrator expresses disgust over the need to walk carefully. Chapter 10 shows this clearly. In his world one must act wisely, cautiously, using wisdom instead of force. One must understand all the details before giving an opinion. One should not open one's mouth unnecessarily, or ever conspire against the king. Any mistake can be fatal. Says Qoheleth: "Do not curse the king, even in your thoughts, or curse the rich, even in your bedroom; for a bird of the air may carry your voice, or some winged creature tell the matter" (10:20).

When the walls have ears, there is no freedom and no serenity. From the viewpoint of survival, and considering that one never knows what will happen, Qoheleth warns against taking extreme decisions; one must guard against evil from every direction. To accept that "a bird in the hand is worth two in the bush" is troublesome to our protagonist; that too is *hebel.*

To be cautious about everything does not lead to happiness; it is *hebel,* but he sees no other way and gives this realistic advice: "In the morning sow your seed, and at evening do not let your hands be idle; for you do not know which will prosper, this or that, or whether both alike will be good" (11:6).

Since both choices have the same value, Qoheleth again discounts the possibility of a better future; if everything is the same, death will come and the days of darkness will be many, for "all that comes is *hebel*" (11:7-8).

Death as the Great Leveler

Qoheleth protests the fact that there are no distinctions on the other side of death. There is no reward or distinction for those who excel in wisdom, wealth, righteousness, or justice; the same fate befalls them all, and there is no enduring remembrance of any of them (2:16). In 2:15 he says: "Then I said to myself, 'What happens to the fool will happen to me also; why then have I been so very wise?' And I said to myself that this also is *hebel.*"

He repeats the same thing more clearly in 9:2. For Qoheleth this is one of the great evils that happen under the sun. Especially because those whose "hearts are full of evil" during their lifetime simply die, as everyone does, without receiving what they deserve (9:3).

Death too, then, is an accomplice of the injustice committed under the sun. In 3:19 he goes so far as to argue that the fate of humans and animals is the same.

Not Finding the Ideal Woman

Qoheleth has had a bad experience with women. He lashes out against the woman who ensnares and suffocates men. She is more bitter than death, he says (7:26). But what his soul still seeks, and has not found, is a woman. Perhaps he is alluding to Genesis 2, in which the Creator makes woman out of Adam's body for the perfection of humanity, and Adam lovingly exclaims: "This at last is bone of my bones and flesh of my flesh" (Genesis 2:23). He does not find this ideal companion, just as he does not find wisdom (Qoheleth 7:23-24); he might find one man among a thousand, but not the woman he idealizes (7:28).

He ends by saying that what he has really found is that God made human beings straightforward, "but they have devised many schemes" (7:29). For Qoheleth, then, the world as *hebel* is not the work of a star-crossed, tragic destiny;[11] rather it is human beings themselves who turned it upside down. An inverted reality complicates the possibility of finding new horizons under the sun.

THE WORLD NOT NARRATED BY QOHELETH: EVERYTHING IS NEW UNDER THE SUN

The Newness of the Hellenistic Period

The world narrated by Qoheleth affirms the absence of newness under the sun; all is *hebel,* rubbish, an emptiness, useless, absurd; that is true even of life because it is ephemeral. Qoheleth relativizes the common theology of the wisdom tradition he has inherited, and also the theology of the messianic promises of the prophets, by pointing out its incongruence with everyday experience. The theoretical schemas of theology do not meet the historical challenges of his time. There is no visible sign of messianic punishment for the wicked or reward for the righteous. There are moments, later in his monologue, when he comes back to that theology—but only after dismantling it, denying its historical truth.

But the real world in which Qoheleth writes is quite the opposite from this narrated world. Everything is new. Although many of the Egyptian and Persian ways have continued, they have been reviewed, reorganized, and made more effective.[12] Analysts of the Hellenistic period say that an amazing, unprecedented structural change was taking place. This was especially so after the death of Alexander the Great, during the Ptolemaic period, when the Book of Ecclesiastes was written (between 280 and 230 B.C.E.).[13]

Under Ptolemaic rule, change was taking place in every field:[14] military tactics, the method of exercising power from Alexandria, the administration of the kingdom and its finances, the minting of coins, management in Egypt and the provinces, agricultural technology,[15] large-scale commerce, and philosophical discussions; some inventions in mathematics and physics from this period are still used today.[16]

Martin Hengel tells us: "Hellenistic civilization did not appear first in art, literature, or philosophy, but in superior military tactics, and especially in the Egyptian sphere of influence, in the perfect and inexorable administration of the state, whose objective was the best possible use of its subjugated territories."[17]

The geographical and economic structure of Ptolemaic Egypt required a well-organized, directed and centralized administrative structure. Under the first Ptolemies, the Greeks embraced the Eastern idea of divinizing the king and applied it in conjunction with Greek logic. The efficiency of the Greeks was added to the absolute power of the king as a god, owner of the land. Thus, the king had an administrator (*dioiketes*), in charge of all the finances and administration of the state.

The Papyri of Zeno, discovered in the early twentieth century, give details of the economic and fiscal administration of the state. One sees there the oppressive agrarian bureaucracy, the monetary problems, the ways of the functionaries, the workings of commerce, and an infinity of family affairs.[18] Apollonius was the *dioiketes*, or administrator, of Ptolemy Philadelphus (in 261 B.C.E.); he received information on everything related to economic production from Zeno, a functionary assigned to the provinces. Each province was visited by two royal functionaries: an economist (*oikonomos*) for the administration of finance and commerce, and a military official (*strategos*); under them was a long list of subordinate officials and a heavy bureaucracy.[19]

According to M. Rostovtzeff, "the prevailing spirit of the Oriental Greeks of that time was one of confidence in the unlimited capacities of man and his reason"; the Greeks were aggressive and audacious, and worked hard to achieve high economic and social levels. It was a time of improvement in business methods, with an increase in banks and credits and an abundance of metal coins; many manuals were also circulated about the scientific use of the land.[20]

In the years 266-259 B.C.E. there was surprising economic and financial activity. Hengel dates its origin to the beginning of Ptolemaic rule. The newness is obvious: "From the beginning, administrative firmness was supplemented by a powerful state commerce, completely new, unknown in any oriental state." Egypt has even been called "a money-making machine."[21]

The Ptolemaic monopoly on coins was a key to their commercial growth. The coins of other independent cities were collected or suspended, and those of the Ptolemies (in gold, silver, and copper) circulated in sufficient quantities.[22] Coins from the time of Ptolemy II have been found in Palestine, showing the commercial boom of the time; they are more common than those of Alexander, Attica, or Phoenicia. According to Hengel, coins were generally substituted for the exchange of goods in Palestine.[23] We might call this the beginning of the new economic order which replaced bartering with monetary exchange.

This situation had negative consequences for non-Greeks. Alexandria, the capital of Egypt, was seen by many Greeks as the promised land, because they had the advantage of not being "barbarians"; but the situation of servants or slaves was quite the opposite. Their conditions were miserable; there are testimonies of slaves who ran away when they learned that they would be taken to Egypt.[24] There are also documents about strikes, protests, and uprisings in Egypt, which were put down by mercenary troops, which suggests unlimited exploitation.[25] Regarding the labor force, Rostovtzeff notes that technical advances in agriculture led to a rapid transformation in which slave labor played a leading role, primitive agricultural and industrial methods were left behind, and independent artisans and domestic manufacturing were swept away by slave labor.[26]

The empire's foreign policy was conducted through relations with the aristocrats of the subjugated provinces, in order to maintain power. They were given religious and cultural but not economic and political freedom. In Palestine the empire relied on nobles and officials, landowning aristocrats and priestly leaders. The family of the Tobiads, who blocked the reform of Esdras and Nehemiah after the return from exile, was represented by Joseph and later his son Hyrcanus, as collaborators of the empire. In the reign of Ptolemy III, Joseph of the Tobiads was charged with collecting taxes in the province as the general overseer.[27] The nonaristocratic Semitic population was simply an object of exploitation, according to Hengel; all that was needed of them was unlimited economic productivity.[28] He also says that a Palestinian peasant complained bitterly to Zeno over the salary promised him; it was often withheld because, according to the papyrus, "they have seen that I am a barbarian, and I do not know how to live like a Greek."[29]

There was newness not only in the foreign rule but also within Palestine. Anna Maria Rizzante and Sandro Gallazzi have pointed out newness in the Jewish world. The fourth and fifth centuries saw the consolidation of the theocratic system that began with the project of Esdras. In the center was the new temple, bringing together all the powers; its instrument was a new, detailed law that distinguished between pure and impure, sacred and profane. And the concentration of income led to a new ritual of sacrifices, vows, and offerings. Economic and ideological domination was focused on "a people made impure by the law, who must therefore pay for their constant need of purification."[30]

This situation of exploitation, aggravated by the implacable collection of high taxes and by the rapid Hellenization of the Jewish aristocracy, was becoming more and more unbearable. The progress and the lack of social concern registered in the years 285-246 B.C.E., led the way to the uprisings of the Maccabees and the growth of apocalyptic consciousness.

The Author in His Context

We can observe three conflicting perceptions of the world. It is a struggle of ideologies. The eye of Qoheleth sees what perhaps many of his compatriots do not see. Some may have become fascinated with the system and with the efficiency of the Greeks;[31] others may have continued repeating their traditional theological schemas, out of touch with reality, perhaps accompanied by the requirements of the law of purification. The world described by Qoheleth, as he sees and examines it from day to day, places his own wisdom tradition in contradiction. His vision goes against that of the Hellenistic Ptolemaic functionaries, as manifested in the surprising power and efficiency of their administration, technology, and production. Qoheleth challenges the newness of the dominant foreign system, perhaps because its impact does not lead to human fulfillment.

The author is in a delicate position. His character rejects the Jewish wisdom tradition as historically unverifiable, and at the same time he rejects the real world ruled by the Ptolemies. The author seems to be going through a crisis of faith, unable to see any utopian possibilities of social organization. There is no feasible macrostructural solution, not even an unfeasible one. He can only recommend living intensely from day to day as an affirmation of life, in order to be happy, and affirming by faith that someday things will be different, for there is a time and a season for everything (3:1-8). We shall return to this point later.

We have two subjects: the narrator, who calls himself Qoheleth, and the author of the text, whom we shall try to identify through his own writings.

The author is not mentioned in any writings outside the text itself, so we know nothing about his personal life in the history that transcends the text. But we can learn something about him and his vision from the way he constructs his narrated universe and his characters.

It has been suggested that, judging by his use of images from the royal court, the author belongs to the Palestinian aristocracy in Jerusalem. More specifically, he would be a sage who imparts his wisdom in the circles of young Jewish aristocrats, warning them against the apparent newness of the Hellenistic system and culture.[32]

His character, Qoheleth, seems to coincide with that position. Qoheleth is presented as a king (1:12-2:10);[33] he is surprised to see princes walk and slaves ride horseback (10:7); and he suggests that the rich should enjoy the wealth that God gave them and not waste their lives working to accumulate wealth (5:19).

If this is so, these subjects (the author and the character) may both be renegade aristocrats. Obviously the author's discourse is not in line with the Hellenistic penetration that appropriates Palestinian land by royal decree and dictates norms from Egypt to its own rulers. It makes no sense to work to exhaustion without taking the time to enjoy the product of one's labor, and to live in permanent risk of losing wealth and land through either confiscation or bad investments. Moreover, the creation of poverty and oppression goes against the religious tradition of his people. The traditional laws of Jubilee for the egalitarian readjustment of the population are not a part of the imperial laws of the foreigners. In Greek history there is nothing like the Jewish prophetic tradition, which favors the poor and oppressed. Hengel recalls that the Greeks recognized a responsibility to one's family and city, but not to one's impoverished fellow citizens.[34]

The author also criticizes his aristocratic contemporaries who are aligned with the imperial power. He is probably referring, as some suggest, to Joseph of the Tobiads—a powerful and rich family from Transjordan, chosen by Ptolemy III to collect the province's taxes and to send them to the royal treasury in Alexandria.[35]

It is interesting that the author, in narrating his world, denies the newness of this unnarrated world. As we have seen, he is writing at a time of great economic and political stability, amid a monetary boom under the first two Ptolemies. Several documents from the Jewish aristocracy refer in a positive tone to that empire.

The Book of Ecclesiastes is evidently a criticism of the imperial power and the Hellenized lifestyle of his aristocratic Jewish compatriots.[36] Why would the author reject the new, if he was not among the most affected members of the population? There are many possible reasons. Either his analysis was very acute, discerning the intentions of the new Hellenistic economic order, and he was right about the negative consequences it would have for his people—especially for the poor among them, or he was simply a xenophobic conservative, distrustful of everything new. I tend toward the first of these interpretations. The document we are analyzing is contentious, "subversive and anti-monarchical."[37]

But that is not the problem that concerns us. Rather it is that the author seems unable to explicitly define a utopia that explains existence as a structure of possibility, moving toward something different from the enslaving toil, the constant self-censorship, the lack of solidarity, and the anxiety over imminent death that he sees, and enabling him to struggle for change. Qoheleth apparently does not have the power that comes from faith in something, which would lead him to a transforming praxis. A "*hebel*ian" atmosphere clouds his horizons.

Later we see him come out of this dilemma, but only in part. On the one hand, he manages to project his inability to see into the future onto a transcendent God, who mysteriously acts and organizes a time for everything; and, on the other hand, he categorically affirms the solution of finding something good in the present and living for it, such as eating and drinking and finding enjoyment in one's toil. This is not for him a realized utopia, because, in his logic, in the end that too is *hebel*, since not everyone can do it; it is also ephemeral, like adolescence and youth (11:10). Everything is *hebel*. Nevertheless, this is the most positive approach from the viewpoint of feasibility. Let us now look more closely at this limited utopia.

THE HIDDEN UTOPIA OF QOHELETH[38]

Let us return to the world that Qoheleth does narrate. I have said that our character sees no future possibility of change; he affirms that there is nothing new under the sun, and that everything is *hebel*. He has analyzed his reality in great detail. He uses different Hebrew words to describe this task. "I said to my heart," which he often uses, means entering into reasoned analysis; the heart in Hebrew (*leb*) is above all an organ of reason.[39] Elsewhere in the text he repeatedly uses the words for wisdom (*hokmah*), knowing (*yadaᶜ*), seeing (*raʾah*), which means examining closely, finding (*matsaʾ*), seeking (*biqesh*), investigating (*tur*), and others. Thus the narrator presents his description of reality as proven truth, using experience as an instrument of knowledge.[40] Qoheleth 7:25 is full of such investigative words: "I turned my mind to know and to search out and to seek wisdom and the sum of things, and to know that wickedness is folly and that foolishness is madness."

Despite this effort he is unable to see what will be. But he does discover a dimension that he had not previously seen as primordial, and he proposes a way to overcome the anguish of the rejected, present situation. That is, as we have already seen, to enjoy the everyday intimacy of life: to eat and drink and find enjoyment in one's toil, "because this too is a gift of God"—the share or portion (*heleq*) that belongs to him. The words "this too" (*gam zoh . . .*) are the counterpart of his constant phrase, "this too is *hebel*" (*gam zeh hebel*). Before going into more detail about this subjective alternative, let us try to unfold the utopia that is implicit, although consciously denied by reason, in the text.

Franz Hinkelammert analyzes neoliberal thinking with its self-proclaimed realism and explicit anti-utopianism, and concludes that it too has a hidden utopia: it repeatedly refers to impossible horizons that transcend the human condition. This leads Hinkelammert to affirm the existence of utopias as a necessary human condition. Therefore, he says, "No human thinking can set itself outside the utopian horizon. Whoever intentionally attempts to think of a 'realism without utopia,' unintentionally reproduces his or her own utopian horizons."[41]

If that is so, our character Qoheleth cannot be anti-utopian or nonutopian, although he seems to be so in affirmations such as "What is crooked cannot be made straight" (1:15; cf. 7:13). In fact he is not, despite the overabundance of his pessimistic judgment. We must also consider that the discourse in the text is a contradictory, typically subjective, monologue. For example, on the one hand, he praises the dead and those not yet born, because they do not see the great violence and injustice committed under the sun (4:2-4); he also considers the stillborn happier than those who have lived two thousand years of toil, without enjoying even one of those years (6:6). On the other hand, he concludes that life is better than death; the dead no longer have a share in the dynamic of life under the sun, for they do not even have love, hate, or envy (9:4-6). In 9:4 he affirms that "a living dog is better than a dead lion."

This is not what we would call an enthusiastic affirmation, sufficient to keep hope alive or the horizon open. We have to approach Qoheleth differently in order to see his utopian horizons. We can do this from three angles. First, from the negative angle: if everything is absurd, what might a non-absurd, a non-*hebel*, look like? This is the level of desires implicit in the rejection of the present. A second level is the utopian horizon of the desire explicit in the affirmation of present, everyday life. A third level is explicit, trusting faith in an all-powerful and unknowable God, who at some time in history will do what human beings cannot do, precisely because they are human.

The Desires Implicit in the Rejection of the Present

We can identify four important desires: for knowledge of the times, for justice and freedom, for happiness, and for the transcendence of death.

The Desire, and Impossibility, of Knowing the Times

One of our character's greatest frustrations is his inability to know the future and to understand the complexity of what is happening in the present under the sun. He cannot understand why the present is *hebel*, and the interpretive schemes of his tradition do not help him understand this reality.

It seems that knowledge is salvation; it is important to know the future in order to make the present "absurdity" bearable and find a place within it. But despite all the efforts of wisdom and science, he cannot know or understand (6:12; 7:24; 8:7). Knowledge and wisdom cause vexation and sorrow (1:17-18); what he finds, as he sees it, is only *hebel*, and he cannot understand what God has done from the beginning to the end (3:11). It surprises him and overwhelms his suppositions. In 8:17 he repeats that despite all his toil in seeking (*ra'ah*), he cannot find out the work of God.

The helplessness of not knowing the times or the divine purpose causes him suffering because he cannot put together a coherent praxis; it diminishes his humanity by blocking his self-fulfillment. He gropes for signs that would show him the way (11:1-6), because one cannot know what disaster may happen on earth (11:2). Qoheleth posits that wisdom is better than wealth and power, among other things, but wisdom also has limits. He criticizes his own wisdom.

Since the narrator cannot objectively control and rationally order the times, he reframes them and moves them beyond his consciousness: he projects them into God's control. The times transcend him; he can only attribute a utopian function to them. This rehumanizes him because it permits him to know his limits, that is, his human condition. The trusting affirmation that there is a time and a season for everything is the utopian, life-ordering phrase. By affirming that fact he can avoid being annihilated by the present. If there is a time to be born and a time to die, to build and to destroy, to laugh and to weep, there must also be a time for *hebel* and a time for non-*hebel*. The newness that Qoheleth himself rejects becomes a proclamation of the time of non-*hebel*. This is utopian, in the sense that it happens independently of human effort.

The Desire for Justice and Freedom in Society

Justice for the poor and oppressed is an implicit desire behind Qoheleth's rejection of the present. That is obvious; the key points of his discourse reveal it. Society is inverted, with wickedness in the place of justice (3:16); power is in the hands of the oppressors; the poor are violently oppressed, and there is no one to comfort their tears (4:1). The state does not fulfill its task of administering justice and social welfare (5:8), and the tyranny of the king is unbearable; no one can reproach him, for he does whatever he pleases as if he were God (8:3-4), and his spies are all around (10:20).

The non-*hebel* society of Qoheleth is where justice, law, and freedom reign. This is his utopia. Since it is not explicit and he does not consider it feasible, not even by means of anticipation, he does not suggest a way of approaching it or a praxis to bring it closer. But here again, he finds a possibility in his faith in a time for everything. That is how I interpret the following verses:

He says of the inverted society: "I said in my heart, God will judge the righteous and the wicked, for he has appointed a time for every matter, and for every work" (3:17).

And he says of the king's tyranny: "For the word of the king is powerful, and who can say to him, 'What are you doing?' Whoever obeys a command will meet no harm, and the wise mind will know the time and way.* For every matter has its time

---

* In the Spanish version used by the author (based on the Reina Valera), "way" (*mishpat* in Hebrew) is rendered as "judgment."

and way, although the troubles of mortals lie heavy upon them. Indeed, they do not know what is to be, for who can tell them how it will be?" (8:4-7). The word "judgment" (*mishpat*) is generally synonymous with justice (*tsedeq*).

As we can see, the structure of possibility comes not from knowledge of the times in a chronological sense but from faith in the existence of a ripe or opportune time; Qoheleth is speaking from a kairological viewpoint.[42]

The Desire for Happiness

The desire for happiness appears explicitly in the refrain, "there is nothing better for mortals than to eat and drink, and find enjoyment in their toil." But it also appears in the rejection of the present toil (*'amal*). Let us look at it from this angle. Such laborious toil to accumulate wealth is worthless, if "I am depriving myself of pleasure," *tob* (4:8), or if one can live two thousand years and yet "enjoy no good," *tob* (6:6).[43] Happiness should go with weary toil; Qoheleth does not reject the process of labor, but rather the enslaving way in which one toils but does not enjoy its product. In 2:10, enjoyment of the product— not money but happiness in the labor process—is the due reward, the share (*heleq*). That is why he recommends moderation in work: "Better is a handful with quiet than two handfuls with toil, and a chasing after wind" (4:6).

Just what does happiness mean for him? He cannot define it here; he only affirms that one should enjoy. Perhaps he means enjoying the chronological time that we live every day, but he is not yet satisfied with respect to the true happiness that embraces long times and short times. Therefore he asks: "For who knows what is good (*tob*) for mortals while they live the few days of their vain life (*hebel*), which they pass like a shadow? For who can tell them what will be after them under the sun?" (6:12).

Here we see clearly Qoheleth's concern over the problem of death.

The Implicit Desire to Transcend Death

Qoheleth sees happiness in the dead and stillborn who are in *sheol,* not because he wishes to be with them—we have already seen that he prefers to be among the living—but because they do not see the oppression and injustice of his world. Our character does not want to die. He doesn't say it this way, but he is angry that both the just and the wicked die, with no distinction between them (9:2-3). Putting his thought in negative terms: for Qoheleth the wicked should die, but not the just. The oppressor spends his life doing evil, and he is not judged but simply dies. The just person does good in his life; his goodness is not recognized; and finally he receives the same reward as the wicked: death. And the living forget the dead.

Then Qoheleth goes further. Death not only levels all human beings of different conditions but also levels beasts with humans (3:20-21). Qoheleth does not formulate a possibility of resurrection, because this discussion had not yet arisen in Judaism in the third century B.C.E. The hopelessness of their situation may have led to its appearance a short time later; the concept appears in the Book of Wisdom (first century B.C.E.).

Death is a misfortune against which all human beings are powerless (8:8). The time of death is described as evil, a time of darkness (11:8). It is also wrong that no one can know when it will happen (9:12).

Since death is a given, uncontestable reality, since no one knows what lies beyond death, and since no one knows when their time will come, Qoheleth accepts it; and by accepting it, he acknowledges his human condition. From that acknowledgment he derives two viable alternatives: not to hasten the time of death by doing things that can cause harm; and to enjoy the present life intensely, especially before old age sets in and announces the inexorable coming of death.

Since his world is *hebel,* it is important to be able to live in it intelligently, discerning the times as best he can. In times of repression one must walk cautiously. Thus he says that in times of prosperity one should enjoy and be happy, and in times of adversity one must reflect and consider (7:14). If society is so inverted that things go badly for the righteous and well for the wicked, then one should be neither too righteous nor too wicked (7:16-19); in an inverted situation, either extreme may lead to premature death. Our character's conclusion must have been surprising in the context of the religious thinking of his time.

This is not an ideal solution. It too is sometimes counted as *hebel;* yet it is the best one can do at a given moment in everyday life, in order to endure the repressive reality and not to die prematurely. It is not a matter of cynicism or indifference, but rather of historical realism in the context of chronological time. The concept of fearing God provides an important protection against frustrating helplessness and thus enables one to enjoy everyday life freely and blamelessly.

The other viable alternative in the struggle against death is to resist the *hebel* of the present time—which is like death—by means of pleasure. This alternative must be implemented before old age saps the energy of life and before death, the world of darkness where there is no life. The context of future, eternal death as the dwelling place of human beings: that too is *hebel* (11:8, cf. 12:5).

His advice is addressed to youth: to make the most of the present, to follow the yearnings of their hearts and their eyes; not to be angry, and to avoid evil (11:9-10); to enjoy their pleasures freely. In this time of enjoyment he advises them to remember the Creator before the world of the present life ends (12:1-2), old age saps their strength (12:3-6), and they die forever (12:7). These pleasures should not be destructive of self or neighbor, Qoheleth is careful to remind them; they should enjoy fully, knowing that God will judge all that they do (11:9). Here God is a symbol of limits, for their own protection.

Qoheleth does not fear the future death, nor does he love it or encourage suicide; he sees it as a reality to be beaten at its own game, by enjoying many days of material happiness before it arrives. Thus he mocks death, although at the end he will have to accept it. Those who do not enjoy life in the midst of so much enslaving toil are letting death win prematurely. Because the opposite of death is not just life, but life lived with pleasure and dignity. It is faith in a time for everything—a time to be born and a time to die—that permits him neither to fear death nor to love it, but to make the most of real life in the time between birth and death.

The Explicit, Feasible Alternative: Affirming Material and Sensual Life in the Everyday World

After examining his world and realistically observing the closing horizons of the near future, Qoheleth's proposed solution is to reject the present without ceasing to affirm the real, sensual life that can be lived in the present. He does not recommend ruminating on memories of good times past, in order to be happy. Neither does he propose to live today on illusions of a better future, knowing that there is a time for everything and that happiness will come in its time. That would mean accepting the present with resignation. His explicit alternative is to live—now, in the midst of *hebel*—something that seems to be non-*hebel:* unlimited happiness, knowing that there is a time and a season for everything.

This is a good, feasible solution. If the future is opaque and the past is alienating, then consciousness must be established in the present. But the present may reveal itself to consciousness as a straitjacket, because there are no explicitly defined utopian horizons or promises made to the ancestors. In this case the only alternatives available in the present would be irony, resignation, suicide—or living fully, according to a logic different from the one imposed by "absurdity," the system of *hebel*.

Let us come back to the alternative of affirming real life in the present, this time in the context of the world not narrated by Qoheleth. The logic of the Hellenistic production system is enslaving toil: the economic and political administration keeps up a dehumanizing rhythm of labor, without concern for the subject of labor, the worker. The religious leaders of his people, the leaders of the temple in Jerusalem, also keep up the rhythm of actions required to fulfill the Mosaic Law and its sacrifices. The blind, obedient subjects of the law are turned into objects. It is no longer their conscience that directs their steps but their conditioning by the Hellenistic Ptolemaic administration and the requirements of the temple rites.

Qoheleth is proposing a different logic, one that follows the heart (the subject's own consciousness) and the eyes (what the subject sees). This logic affirms the person as subject. The best way to follow this logic is not to live according to a coherent rationality, which is impossible in his time; this rationality only makes clear the negative, irrational character of the present *hebel*. A better logic for dealing with *hebel* is to affirm life by eating bread and drinking wine with enjoyment, with the person one loves, and in the midst of enslaving toil. This is the central meaning of that phrase, which he repeats six times.[44] It is the unifying theme of his discourse: Qoheleth works, acts, examines, reflects, seeks, and comes to the conclusion that there is nothing better than this everyday activity. Each repetition of the refrain includes different details; the last one gives it its most complete form (9:7-10).

The utopia of everyday enjoyment is a viable, humanizing way of repudiating the present but at the same time living it by a contrary logic. That is, to live as human beings who feel that they are alive, in a society that does not allow them to live because of its demands for productivity and efficiency.

In other appearances of the refrain (2:24-26), he says that this is from the hand of God. That means that the subject can enjoy life without feelings of guilt. The Mosaic Law, interpreted by the temple leaders, constantly demanded rites of purification. Qoheleth follows a different logic, and he makes it even clearer in 9:7-9, saying: "God has long ago approved what you do." In a non-*hebel* world, freedom is absolute. This is only possible because it takes place in a joyful world of shared intersubjectivity, guided not by the law but by a logic that recognizes the subject independently of the law.

This is the explicit utopia of Qoheleth, although by denying that there is anything new in historical times, he fails to recognize it as such. But precisely because it is a utopia, it cannot be fully realized in history, for all human beings.[45] Indeed one cannot always enjoy life, as Qoheleth advises us to do.

But he expresses that desire poetically and symbolically,[46] in the context of his reality. In the reality of foreign domination, everything—production, commerce, meritocracy and war—demands efficiency, without concern for human beings, especially agricultural workers, whether slave or free. And in the local reality, the temple demands sacrifices for purification and for the fulfillment of the law.

Now, not everyone has the resources to eat and drink and a loved one with whom to enjoy life. These are Qoheleth's desires, expressed not in the subjunctive but in the imperative: "Go, eat your bread with enjoyment!" Indeed, it is a right of all human beings, not only a gift of God. Qoheleth calls it our share, or lot (*heleq*), our payment for weary toil (5:18). The real world is *hebel* for this narrator, because the laborer cannot enjoy the product of labor; someone else enjoys it, and that is *hebel*. Non-*hebel* is to enjoy one's own work.

Qoheleth goes further: in search of universality he addresses everyone, including the rich (5:19). To the rich he also suggests enjoying their possessions, because they do not know how to enjoy in this world of *hebel*, or because someone else may take them, or they may invest badly in an unstable market, or because they are too concerned with accumulating more wealth. This way of life does not allow them to know the joy of everyday life, or to share their bread. They do not see themselves as human beings more important than wealth.

The utopian horizon of Qoheleth is that everyone should be able to enjoy material life and, above all, that they know how to enjoy it.

But it is also true—and important—that the alternative of enjoying bodily life without anxiety, amid the rigors of the chronological times and watchfulness for the demands of the law, does not mean proposing a parallel, irresponsible energy at the service of the dehumanizing efficiency of the Ptolemaic machinery, or in subjection to the dictates of the law. It is not a matter of enjoying life by indifferently turning one's back on the dehumanizing devastation of the power of his time. Neither is it inspired by feelings of helplessness, cynicism, and unconcern for the most fragile victims of the prevailing economic policies.

Qoheleth says clearly that one should celebrate life joyfully in the midst of enslaving toil, in the midst of "the absurdity," the *hebel*. This, I believe, is the great challenge and threat to those who deny the dignity and fullness of life. There are grounds for this interpretation in the glyphic art of ancient Mesopotamia: in some scenes sacred banquets were celebrated in the midst of funerals, with music, dancing, drinking, and people making love.[47] In this sense Qoheleth's proposal in an everyday context takes on a larger meaning for the economic-political-religious macrostructure. It is not, then, a matter of trying to approach utopia by creating a parallel community, isolated from and unharmed by the world of *hebel*.

In the final analysis, and perhaps unconsciously, Qoheleth is challenging the logic of "the absurdity" by living within it by the logic of "non-absurdity": by eating bread, drinking wine, and enjoying life with a loved one. Curiously, where previously his failure to know the times dehumanized him by paralyzing him, now with this proposal the opaqueness of the horizon humanizes him: it returns him to himself, to take pleasure in his body and to share his bodily being. And he can affirm himself as a subject in the everyday world, by affirming his faith that there is a time and a season for everything.

The Unfeasible Alternative: Trusting Faith in an All-powerful God

Qoheleth's frustration is his helplessness in the face of *hebel* in the world around him. The key words in the opening poem (1:4-11) imply the presence of a self-regulating machinery that will not allow interference. In this world, everyday events are not taken into account and do not affect the almost perfect functioning of the monotonous events of the universe. Everything is *hebel*, and nothing can be done against it: "I saw all the deeds that are done under the sun; and see, all is vanity and a chasing after wind. What is crooked cannot be made straight, and what is lacking cannot be counted" (1:14-15).

Let us now try to observe the change in Qoheleth's consciousness as he comes to understand the meaningless events and the theological reading that helps him to read the times, which permits him to survive and live well. These changes, of course, are not evolutionary.[48]

To search out by wisdom what happens under the sun is a painful task that God has given to human beings (1:13). This wise understanding of "the madness and folly" causes "vexation and sorrow" (1:17-18). That is because human beings cannot fully understand the absurdity of reality, the great emptiness, the *hebel*. The old, inherited wisdom is that God made everything beautiful and good, and made human beings good. His experience of the world contradicts that premise from every angle. Qoheleth does not understand, and he universalizes his lack of understanding: God made everything beautiful, but human beings do not understand the complete work of God from the beginning to the end, even though God put in their hearts the ability to understand (3:11). No matter how he tries, even though he is wise, he cannot understand the designs of God in history (8:17).

Our narrator does not understand, so he continues his theological reasoning: God made human beings straightforward, but they turned the situation upside down. This is a step toward understanding the events of his world. But he still cannot understand the work of God, for God's omniscience makes God responsible for all that happens under the sun: so God is responsible for Qoheleth's miserable world. In 7:13 it is God who has made things crooked: "who can make straight what he has made crooked?" God is responsible for the fact that some can enjoy the product of their labor and others cannot. This is described as a heavy and grievous ill (6:1-2).

At some point Qoheleth's reasoning reaches its limit: God is God and the human being is a human being. God is stronger; one cannot quarrel with divinity. He presents this as a known fact, without mystery: "Whatever has come to be has already been named, and it is known what human beings are, and that they are not able to dispute with those who are stronger" (6:10). At this point the narrator expresses his helplessness in the face of transcendence and divinity. Curiously, by taking this step of acknowledging his helplessness, he turns it around: his spirit is energized, and he sees the possibility of historicizing the ideal of enjoying life now, in the midst of *hebel*. This is the necessary step that enables him to reconstruct his consciousness and to reorganize his world from a perspective beyond the anguish, desire, and overwhelming agony of *hebel*. This is where the dimension of fearing God comes in (5:7), which is "the beginning of wisdom" in Proverbs, and "the whole duty of everyone" (12:13) according to the appendix of our text, which was written by a later hand (12:9-14).

The term "to fear God" (*yare*), does not mean to be afraid of God. Here in Qoheleth it means, rather, recognizing the distance that separates God from human beings[49]—recognizing God's extraordinary, numinous aspect, which overwhelms human beings because it is inscrutable, unpredictable, an undecipherable enigma. God is mystery. God sets the limits of human potential. Like a mirror or a clear fountain, God makes God's creatures see their human condition. In this sense, to acknowledge God as God is the beginning of human fulfillment. We can live and plan our life, because whatever happens, we have faith that God is there.

Thus, paradoxically, the fear of God means "do not be afraid"; it invites one to be calm in the midst of frenzied praxis. The fear of God is related to human behavior and attitudes toward life; thus it implies a strong note of trust.[50] Acknowledging human limits, consciousness unfolds within the margins of possibility; for God will take charge of the impossible, sometimes through God's subjects. Everything is in God's hands, even though the mystery remains (9:1).

It is helplessness that thrusts human beings into the dimension of faith. Faith, in turn, gives the human being energy for life. As we have seen, Qoheleth reorients the world toward non-

hebel by putting it in God's time. If the time of *hebel* neutralized or paralyzed him, he is liberated by faith that there is a time and a season for everything. God is in control of the times, and it will go well for those who fear God—that is, for those who recognize their limits. This is the power of faith, although Qoheleth does not experience it in the present moment. He has faith that God will act and judge with justice, in the opportune time (3:17-18; 8:12-13; 12:14).

When he reaches this point, Qoheleth's explicit alternative becomes viable: to affirm real life in the joy of eating bread and drinking wine and enjoying the company of the loved one. This is not a matter of irresponsibility or of indifference to the exploitation that takes place under the sun. We are taking sides with life, because we rest in God's grace in the midst of enslaving toil, and against its anti-human logic.

Let us now turn to an analysis of the discourse. As the reader may already have noted, the overall view presented in this introduction is a key to the reading which will give cohesion to our interpretation of the text.[51]

Commentary

The Prologues

At the beginning of the work we find two prologues, and at the end two epilogues, in a chiastic (X-shaped) placement. In both places the narrator is identified, and in both there is an expression of total frustration.

PRESENTATION OF THE NARRATOR (1:1)

[1] The words of the Teacher, the son of David, king in Jerusalem.

"The words of . . ." is a formula commonly used to present a book.[1] Some versions translate the Hebrew Qoheleth as "Preacher," which does not have the same meaning as Teacher but approaches it in one sense: "one who argues." The word, which comes from the Hebrew root *qhl* (assembly), may mean one who calls an assembly, who is in an assembly, or who disputes or argues.[2] Many commentators refer to the Book of Ecclesiastes (a Greek term) as Qoheleth (a Hebrew term). The name Qoheleth is truly an enigma, as Gianfranco Ravasi says. It appears seven times in the book; it is in a feminine form; it is sometimes used with the article "the" as if it referred to a profession, and sometimes without, as a personal name.[3]

In 1:1 the narrator is given the identity of a king,[4] a descendant of David. Obviously the kingly identification is a literary artifice, since there is no known Qoheleth among the kings of Israel or Judah. In identifying him with the son of David there is an implicit allusion to the wise one, Solomon, famous for his wisdom and riches; he is the only known son of King David. Moreover, the story related in 2:4-8 picks up on the actions and attitudes of Solomon as told in 1 Kings 10:23-27 and 2 Chronicles 9:22-27. Referring to Solomon is known as a common ancient way of conferring authority on a writing.

33

The narrator is presented personally as "king over Israel in Jerusalem" in 1:12-2:10, but this never appears again in the book. The final epilogue (12:9-10), which again mentions Qoheleth, presents him simply as a wise teacher.

TOTAL FRUSTRATION (1:2)

[2]Vanity of vanities, says the Teacher, vanity of vanities! All is vanity.

The discourse is framed at the beginning (1:2) and the end (12:8) with a negative statement in superlative form.[5] The most commonly accepted versions translate the Hebrew word *hebel* as "vanity." "Vanity of vanities" is a translation of the superlative in 1:2 and 12:8. The construction of the phrase is typical in Hebrew, indicating the absolute or maximum.[6]

There is consensus among biblical commentators that the word "vanity" is not an exact translation of what our character means. The literal meaning of the Hebrew *hebel* is "puff," "breath," or "breeze." But this literal meaning appears only in Isaiah 57:13. So the word has generally acquired a secondary meaning;[7] its exact nuance depends on the context. It can mean "emptiness," "puff," "vapor," "flightiness," "inconsistency," "inefficiency," "fraud." False gods are sometimes called *hebel* (Jeremiah 2:5; 8:19; 14:22). In Qoheleth it represents a negative judgment, based on experience.[8]

No matter how we translate the word—as "emptiness," "vapor," "mystery,"[9] "the absurd," "illusion," "vanity," or "rubbish"—Qoheleth's evaluation is the result of his disillusionment.[10] I follow Michael V. Fox in believing that the broadest meaning, which embraces almost all the nuances that appear in the book, is "the absurd" in its oppressive and tragic sense.[11] Qoheleth is hoping for one outcome in a particular situation, and he gets a different one. This causes frustration.

Hebel is a favorite word of Qoheleth. It appears five times in the eight-word verse 1:2, and thirty-eight times in the whole book.

SECTION I

Total Frustration under the Sun
(1:3-2:26)

This section introduces the reader to a world of frustration, sorrow, and despair. The whole book is marked by this view of the world, beginning here with startling affirmations (1:2, 11); rhetorical questions with negative answers (1:3, 9-10; 2:2, 12, 15, 22); and an incisive poem depicting the forceful rhythm of nature and history, as a machine that will not allow interference (1:4-8); and as an irrefutable experience (2:26).

Human beings are disregarded in the demanding economic system of the Ptolemies and paralyzed in the face of closed horizons. The narrator sees no real possibilities of change or newness under the sun that would redirect history according to a more human logic. Instead, it seems that the chronological times (past, present, and future) have conspired against humanity by denying human beings any newness in the present, hiding from them the memory of God the liberator from Egyptian slavery, and concealing the promise of a messianic future.

Here in this first section the narrator forces the reader to feel his anguish in the face of the closed horizons.

THE MACHINE THAT WILL NOT
ALLOW INTERFERENCE (1:3-11)

There Is No Human Fulfillment in Enslaving Toil (1:3)

> [3] *What do people gain from all the toil*
> *at which they toil under the sun?*

35

The underlying question that leads Qoheleth to analyze reality is raised at the beginning of his discourse (1:3) and repeated elsewhere (2:22; 3:9). There are three key words in this rhetorical question: gain (*yitron*), toil (*'amal*), and under the sun. The terms reappear frequently throughout the narrative. This suggests the concern that demands an honest analysis of reality. Graham Ogden calls it a programmatic question; it is the leitmotif of the discourse.[1]

Qoheleth wants to know if there is any advantage in human labor. In Hebrew the word *yitron* means advantage, benefit, gain, profit. It occurs ten times in Qoheleth, and nowhere else.[2] It was a late addition to the Hebrew vocabulary, commonly used at the time for mercantile transactions in which an accounting was made and a balance drawn between profit and loss. We recall that in this Hellenistic period commerce was at its height, and there were even manuals on how to do business.

But here the meaning of the word has something to do with an additional advantage.[3] Clearly Qoheleth is not interested in increasing people's economic profit. On the contrary, he relativizes wealth (5:10 [Heb. 5:9]),[4] because the desire for profit diminishes the enjoyment of life (cf. 4:8). The advantage he seeks is true human fulfillment in the labor process and its fruits, in history, under the sun. This question, together with the verses that follow, presuppose a negative answer.

The word *'amal* (labor, work) is a key to Qoheleth's feelings of frustration.[5] He complains repeatedly about wearisome labor. This term means "labor," and at the same time "weariness": *'amal* is both work and the exhaustion that comes from it. Our word "enslaving" reflects this double meaning; it does not refer only to the work of slaves.

In the Hebrew Bible, especially before the exile, *'amal* meant misfortune, harm, oppression, injustice. This was how enemies behaved;[6] in postexilic times it was generally used to describe labor. Perhaps the change occurred because the Ptolemaic empire's great demand for agricultural production, with its wearisome and unprofitable labor, was creating an unbearable situation. Qoheleth is emphasizing the negative connotations of labor.[7]

"Under the sun" simply means "in the world," "on earth," in human history. It is a common expression in the Near East. It appears in the *Gilgamesh Epic*, in two Phoenician funeral inscriptions, and it was used by Euripides and Homer.[8] Elsewhere in the Hebrew Bible it appears as "under heaven," with the same meaning. Qoheleth also uses the latter (1:13; 2:3; 3:1), but his distinctive phrase is "under the sun" (twenty-nine times). For Sandro Gallazzi, the sun means something more than the star that gives light: he sees in it a symbol of the Greco-Roman empire.[9] For Qoheleth, in short, "under the sun" is the historical and cosmic space in which the events of an inverted society, described as absurd *hebel*, take place.

Thus Qoheleth opens his discourse with this triad in 1:3 (gain, wearisome labor, and world), "which summarizes its ethical, anthropological, and cosmic dimensions."[10]

There Is No Human Fulfillment in a World without Purpose (1:4-11)

> [4] *A generation goes, and a generation comes,*
> *but the earth remains forever.*
> [5] *The sun rises and the sun goes down,*
> *and hurries to the place where it rises.*
> [6] *The wind blows to the south,*
> *and goes around to the north;*
> *round and round goes the wind,*
> *and on its circuits the wind returns.*
> [7] *All streams run to the sea,*
> *but the sea is not full;*
> *to the place where the streams flow,*
> *there they continue to flow.*
> [8] *All things are wearisome;*
> *more than one can express;*
> *the eye is not satisfied with seeing,*
> *or the ear filled with hearing.*
> [9] *What has been is what will be,*
> *and what has been done is what will be done;*

> *there is nothing new under the sun.*
> [10] *Is there a thing of which it is said,*
>   *"See, this is new?"*
> *It has already been,*
>   *in the ages before us.*
> [11] *The people of long ago are not remembered,*
>   *nor will there be any remembrance*
>   *of people yet to come*
>   *by those who come after them.*

These verses invite us to pause in our own time, and reflect on the meaning of life in our own particular situation. To that end the author describes the rhythm of the cosmos and human history, as he perceives it. The four elements he uses—the earth, the sun, the winds and the seas—seem to represent the basic elements of Greek cosmogony. His use of participles suggests a continuing action.[11] In vv. 4-7 there are fourteen verbs of movement. We repeatedly see the verbs to go, to turn, to arrive, and to return, but the final image appears to stand still, like the blades of a fan at high speed.

Over against the instability of the generations (vv. 4a, 11) Qoheleth sets the stability of the cosmos. But instability and stability become one in the lack of a clear and satisfying goal. Nothing is guaranteed by implacable activity; the rivers keep running to the sea, but the sea is never filled.

There is a cyclical movement, described with negative connotations, both in the generations and in the cosmos.[12] From his frustrating historical experience, Qoheleth perceives the cosmos as a cosmic machine that will not allow interference. The cosmic (like the economic) system sweeps away the subjectivity of human beings. Human consciousness can never get in its way. Qoheleth is unable to feel the soft sea breeze, or passionately admire a sunset or sunrise.

Verse 8 presents certain difficulties of interpretation. The second part seems out of phase with the whole, as if human beings were always inclined to see and hear from a positive viewpoint. But the first line, "all things are wearisome," follows the tone of monotony and dissatisfaction set in v. 7. Verse 8 as a whole should probably be read in that context.

Verse 8 alludes to the human ability to speak, see, and hear. The generations (*dor*) in v. 4 are seen as real human beings with mouths, eyes, and ears. And just as nature moves without ceasing, the eye is not satisfied with seeing, or the ear with hearing. This is so if we understand that the preceding phrase ("more than one can express") goes with "all things are wearisome."

In the Hebrew, "more than one can express" literally means "a man cannot say" or "no one can say." Since there is no preposition to link it to the preceding phrase (all things are wearisome) or to the one that follows (the eye is not satisfied with seeing), the meaning of these phrases depends on the linkage one reads into it. In one reading, no one can say that the eye is not satisfied with seeing, nor the ear with hearing. This affirmation also makes sense in the text, since monotony causes malaise in one's life, when one loses interest in seeking newness under the sun.

But the three negative phrases can also be linked as parallel phrases by their structure.[13] A human being cannot speak, an eye is not satisfied with seeing, and an ear is not filled with hearing. By its equivalent position, the first phrase would have a meaning similar to the other two. That is, the mouth cannot say enough, just as the eyes cannot see or the ears hear enough.[14]

So whichever interpretation we choose, the verse is describing a total dissatisfaction. Either because one is never satisfied but continues searching fruitlessly or because one has seen and heard everything, so that the eye and the ear give up all hope of finding newness.

From another angle: the Hebrew *dbarym* can mean either "words" or "things." If in v. 8 *dbarym* is translated as "words," it would suggest that all the words have been used and there is nothing left to say.[15] In some cultures, there is a startling similarity between "word" and "thing" or "event." In Genesis 1 the word (of God) has the power to create; when God says "let there be light," the light appears. In the mythology of the Venezuelan Makiritare, thinking and dreaming have the same function.[16] But in Qoheleth's world, words have been emptied by use; they cannot create anything new.

Here perhaps, in addition to criticism of the Ptolemaic system, there is also a veiled criticism of the traditional wisdom, in the sense that the appropriate word for the occasion is not spoken, the observations gathered from experience are incomplete, and what is heard (teachings) is not enough.[17] Or in the sense that whatever is said, seen, and heard does not lead to anything new; it only causes malaise.

In vv. 9-10 Qoheleth turns to historical events. The phrase "under the sun," from v. 3, reappears. Like the earth, events under the sun are perennially fixed. Present, past, and future pass as the generations do, but the events are the same. Qoheleth denies the possibility of anything new. For him there are no motivating, heavenly times nor feasible promises by which to reorganize human consciousness in the present.

The fundamental problem is the loss of historical memory (v. 11). Generations come and go without conserving their own history, which means the death of their peoples. Thus each generation must confront its own present and its meaning.

Vittoria D'Alario visualizes the circular structure of the text in this way:[18]

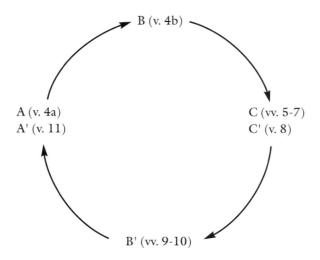

B (v. 4b)

A (v. 4a)
A' (v. 11)

C (vv. 5-7)
C' (v. 8)

B' (vv. 9-10)

Verse 4a describes the cyclical movement of human life; the generations come and go, they are born and die, without interruption and without purpose. Verse 4b affirms the permanence of the earth. Verses 5-7, on the movement of the sun, the wind, and the water, describe the cyclical movement of nature. In v. 8, human dissatisfaction is like the dissatisfaction of the sea, the sun, and the wind. Verses 9-10 emphasize the permanence of that dissatisfaction in all times, and v. 11 shows the loss of memory, present and future, in every generation.

Thus, from the key words in the text we see these two realities —human history and the cosmos—as an implacable, monotonous, totally purposeless activity. Gianfranco Ravasi says of it: "On this road there is no projection, no future, no meaning, no salvation."[19] Subjectivity is absent. The circular structure of the poem also suggests the absence of any possibility of human fulfillment.

Throughout his discourse, conditioned by this introduction, Qoheleth wanders around looking for possible solutions in the present with all its frustration. As we shall see, he is never resigned to this anti-human present.

Costa Rican poet Fernando Contreras Castro has penetrated the monotonous cosmos of our time, at the end of the second millennium. But to his eyes the sun seems tired, not unwearied as in 1:5: "More out of habit than from any world-organizing principle, the sun began to rise, clinging to the hill as in the last effort of a mountain-climber, dangling over the abyss of the night before."[20]

The same poet also speaks of generations: generations of garbage-pickers, who are called divers: "The imperceptible yawn of the flies and the fleet of vultures stretching their wings meant nothing new to the early-morning divers."

There is nothing new, for it is what one sees every day in the underworld, where people struggle daily for the spoils of the vultures and the "divers" in a sea of garbage: "Between the persistent drizzle and the vapors rising from that endless sea, the last trucks, now empty, moved away to begin another day of collection."

In the narrated world of Contreras we find what people experience as *hebel* in daily life: waiting for garbage, seeing garbage arrive, choosing garbage, selling garbage, eating and wearing garbage. . . . But incredible as it may seem, in this garbage-world it is also possible to find tender and true love, like the love of Unica, Contreras's main character.[21]

THE FRUSTRATING EXPERIENCE OF THE SAGE, THE PARTY-GOER, AND THE LABORER (1:12-2:26)

The general affirmations of the preceding verses are incontestably based on personal experience, to which the narrator now refers. He does so in the first person, in order to prove that his discourse is not built out of someone else's abstract philosophical ideas, but has emerged from his own experience. The narrator of our story is also the protagonist.

The narrator, identifying himself as a wise, rich king with the power to fulfill all his own desires, bitterly expounds on his disillusionment with the practice of wisdom, pleasure, and above all with enslaving toil—when the product of his toil is enjoyed by others who did not work. In a fast-paced system that does not lead to human fulfillment because it will not allow interference, because people appropriate the labor of others and there is no possibility of newness or change, there is nothing to be gained by knowledge, pleasure, or labor. Reality becomes painfully incomprehensible and hateful.

But Qoheleth does not let his discourse end there. In 2:24 he introduces a small possibility of life worth living, which he explores later on. Despite the total frustration of this world under the sun, there is a gift from God which may be meaningful in the midst of frustration: to eat and drink, and to enjoy the fruit of one's labor.

This section opens with an introduction (1:12-15) that warns about the hard task of trying to understand what happens under the sun. Then it takes up the following themes: experience with wisdom (1:16-18), experience with pleasures and the self-enhancement that comes from works (2:1-11); death, which does not distinguish between the wise and the foolish (2:12-17); the frustration of not benefiting from one's toil (2:18-23); and the possibility of enjoying everyday life in the midst of labor (2:24-26).

The Frustration of Searching for Wisdom, Knowing in Advance That "What Is Crooked Cannot Be Made Straight" (1:12-15)

> *12I, the Teacher, when king over Israel in Jerusalem, 13applied my mind to seek and to search out by wisdom all that is done under heaven; it is an unhappy business that God has given to human beings to be busy with. 14I saw all the deeds that are done under the sun; and see, all is vanity and a chasing after wind.*
>
> *15 What is crooked cannot be made straight, and what is lacking cannot be counted.*

Two elements lend authority to the narrator's declarations about the absurdity of reality: his use of the first person singular and his identity as a king. The first refers to his personal experience, the second to his ability to do whatever he wants. He is speaking in a literary context. There is no reference to a king named Qoheleth in the Hebrew historical tradition. Wisdom teachings were often attributed to royalty in the ancient Orient, especially in Egypt.[22]

Qoheleth picks up that literary custom in this section of his discourse, because it gives him authority to speak of riches and power. Only a king can satisfy his unlimited desires. King Solomon, as a figure famed for his wisdom, wealth, and luxury, fits perfectly with the character that Qoheleth wishes to represent to the reader. But against all expectations, this character clearly establishes the limits of wisdom. In fact, this is a self-criticism: with the authority of a famous sage, he criticizes those who believe that they can transform the world with their wisdom.[23]

With profound honesty Qoheleth sets out to understand the events of his reality, "everything that happens under the sun," by wisdom. His intention is to focus all the efforts of knowledge on penetrating the enigma of the events of his world. Four words suggest the intensity of this purpose: he turns his heart (*leb*) (NRSV: mind) to seek (*darash*), to spy or investigate (*tur*) (NRSV: search out),[24] and wisdom (*hokmah*). The word for heart (*leb*) appears often in Qoheleth's discourse; to the Hebrews it meant, above all, the center of the intellect. Wisdom (*hokmah*) in Hebrew refers to practical knowledge; it connotes ability or intelligence.

This is a business that humans must carry out, for it is given by God. The word "God" appears here for the first time. Qoheleth chooses the term *ᵓelohim*, which is generally used in the wisdom literature, because of its universality. He does not use Yahweh, the name for God that is more often identified with the liberation history of the Hebrews.

This is a difficult and painful occupation, a "wretched business,"[25] not only because his world is incomprehensible, but because it is frustrating and painful to know that what is crooked cannot be made straight and what is lacking cannot be counted.

In v. 14 Qoheleth anticipates the result of this dogged effort: all that happens under the sun is absurd (*hebel*), impossible to understand or to control. The Hebrew word *rᶜut* means to shepherd or to hunt; the direct object is wind (*ruah*). Thus *rᶜut ruah* means either to shepherd the wind, or to hunt the wind. In the former he would be saying that events under the sun cannot be controlled;[26] a shepherd can control the sheep or goats, but not the wind. In the latter he would be describing a totally useless effort, since no one can catch the wind. We can combine this term with the frustrating, painful psychological experience of not finding what one searches for. *Rᶜut ruah* appears nine times in the book; seven times in combination with *hebel*, absurd. It intensifies the speaker's emotional feeling.[27] The

Reina Valera translation, following the Vulgate, renders *rᶜut ruah* as "affliction of spirit"; this suggests the suffering of one who describes his world as *hebel.*

In 1:15 Qoheleth quotes a proverb, in a synonymous parallel that summarizes the impossibility of changing the course of history. A saying from Latin American popular wisdom reflects the meaning of the first part: "A crooked seedling never becomes a straight tree."

The Pain of Knowing for Certain
What Is Crooked (1:16-18)

> ¹⁶*I said to myself, "I have acquired great wisdom, surpassing all who were over Jerusalem before me; and my mind has had great experience of wisdom and knowledge."* ¹⁷*And I applied my mind to know wisdom and to know madness and folly. I perceived that this also is but a chasing after wind.*
> ¹⁸ *For in much wisdom is much vexation,*
> *and those who increase knowledge increase sorrow.*

Here Qoheleth repeats what he said in 1:12-15 about his frustrating experience as a wise man. Now he further dramatizes it. He boasts of his great wisdom and knowledge, zealously acquired, but only to disclose their limitations. To be wise but unable to do anything fills one with anguish, and the more wisdom and knowledge one has, the greater is the suffering and sorrow.

Qoheleth is probably alluding to his inverted society, where wickedness is handed down instead of justice (3:16); where it is better not to be born, so as not to see the oppression of the poor (4:3). Says James L. Crenshaw: "Open eyes see the injustice of society, and it is disturbing to be aware of oppression and of the absurdity of life."[28]

The Latin American saying "What the eyes do not see, the heart does not feel" expresses this meaning with respect to faithful or unfaithful love. But one cannot be unseeing with respect to reality in general. One must know, no matter how much suffering it causes; anguish and indignity can lead to a transforming praxis. Qoheleth is engaged in this search for something new and satisfying "under the sun."

To know wisdom, to understand madness and folly, is an attempt to embrace history in all its dimensions.

Unlimited Pleasure and Unceasing Self-enhancement Activity Are Not the Best Options (2:1-11)

> 2^1 I said to myself, "Come now, I will make a test of pleasure; enjoy yourself." But again, this also was vanity. ^{2} I said of laughter, "It is mad," and of pleasure, "What use is it?" ^{3} I searched with my mind how to cheer my body with wine—my mind still guiding me with wisdom—and how to lay hold on folly, until I might see what was good for mortals to do under heaven during the few days of their life. ^{4} I made great works; I built houses and planted vineyards for myself; ^{5} I made myself gardens and parks, and planted in them all kinds of fruit trees. ^{6} I made myself pools from which to water the forest of growing trees. ^{7} I bought male and female slaves, and had slaves who were born in my house; I also had great possessions of herds and flocks, more than any who had been before me in Jerusalem. ^{8} I also gathered for myself silver and gold and the treasure of kings and of the provinces; I got singers, both men and women, and delights of the flesh, and many concubines.
>
> ^{9} So I became great and surpassed all who were before me in Jerusalem; also my wisdom remained with me. ^{10} Whatever my eyes desired I did not keep from them; I kept my heart from no pleasure, for my heart found pleasure in all my toil, and this was my reward for all my toil. ^{11} Then I considered all that my hands had done and the toil I had spent in doing it, and again, all was vanity and a chasing after wind, and there was nothing to be gained under the sun.

Qoheleth's subjective dissatisfaction is great. How can one attain self-fulfillment in a world where human beings are not recognized as being human and cannot meaningfully intervene in history? In 1:12-18 Qoheleth tried to understand the events of his reality through wisdom; his only reward was suffering, because he understood that "what is crooked cannot be made straight." Now, in 2:1-11, he tries other ways: ways that diminish awareness by means of pleasure and activity. But vv. 1 and 11 portray the fruitless results. There is no human fulfillment in unlimited personal pleasure, nor in great activity for self-enhancement. It is all absurd, there are no goals to achieve; no purpose is truly worth taking on with integrity, in either pleasure or labor.

He makes a conscious choice ("I searched with my mind," without giving up wisdom in my mind) to take the opposite way from wisdom, that is, folly. His concern is to discover happiness, the good (*tob*) that should occupy human beings during their existence. To that end he cheers his body with wine, with the immense happiness that comes from wine, and with frenzied, self-centered activity to satisfy his unlimited desires. Both activities act as a drug. Perhaps he will find happiness in alienation, by withdrawing from the world that does not allow him to be.

Verses 4-10 are a fast-paced description of the incessant activity of the self, for the self. I made great works, I built, I planted, I made for myself, I bought, I had, I prospered, I did not keep back. While the cosmos implacably follows its rhythm (cf. 1:4-7), the self sets out to do the same.

But the self does not get what it wants. Even when it has surpassed everyone else, and has not denied itself anything that catches its eye, it has not found full happiness or the desired fulfillment (v. 11). Perhaps because it was only for the self, without considering the you or the us or the they. Qoheleth could not think of the other, because his consciousness was drunk on wine and unreflecting activism.

In spite of this selfishness, he did find something that, if only briefly, made him feel that he existed: he found pleasure in what he was doing (2:10). The wisdom he retained (2:9) in the midst of his drunkenness of pleasure and doing led him to reflect that this pleasure was his reward, his portion.[29] It came not from objects or accumulation, but from the joy of doing.

To set the stage for the experience of the self, the narrator uses part of the legend of Solomon in 1 Kings 6:9. Buildings, plantations, gardens, vineyards, pools, slaves, animals, riches, tribute from subjected peoples, singers, women, and music are all part of the Solomonic world.

Qoheleth's criticism of the wise king Solomon is obvious from these frustrating results. But Qoheleth was probably not thinking literally of the legendary king, but rather of the rich aristocratic families of the Jerusalem of his time. What is more, since in v. 8 he mentions having gathered silver and gold and the treasure of kings and provinces, he may also have been thinking of the actions of the Hellenistic overseers of his time.[30]

Is It Worth It to Be Wise in a World That Will Not Allow Interference? (2:12-17)

> [12]So I turned to consider wisdom and madness and folly; for what can the one do who comes after the king? Only what has already been done. [13]Then I saw that wisdom excels folly as light excels darkness.
> [14]The wise have eyes in their head,
>   but fools walk in darkness.
> Yet I perceived that the same fate befalls all of them. [15]Then I said to myself, "What happens to the fool will happen to me also; why then have I been so very wise?" And I said to myself that this also is vanity. [16]For there is no enduring remembrance of the wise or of fools, seeing that in the days to come all will have been long forgotten. How can the wise die like fools? [17]So I hated life, because what is done under the sun was grievous to me; for all is vanity and a chasing after wind.

After reflecting on his experiences with wisdom, pleasures, and incessant labor, Qoheleth—under the pseudonym of the wise king—comes back to the analysis of wisdom and madness-folly.[31] These are the two opposite ways of conducting one's life. He wants to see what will happen, in order to draw a balance and decide whether or not it is worthwhile to conduct one's life wisely in a world that offers no room for human fulfillment. He is interested in the "after" of his present works, so zealously carried out. In v. 11 he has already considered the works of his hands and found them frustrating, but he has not said why. Now he looks at his actions with the future in mind. He is thinking about death. He brings this in gradually. He mentions death euphemistically in v. 12, when he speaks of the one who comes after the king; in vv. 14 and 15, with the "fate" that befalls everyone; in v. 16b, with the "days to come." Then he mentions it bluntly in v. 16c: "the wise die just like fools."

In truth his underlying concern is not with his own death, but with the future of the present situation. Is it worth it to make the effort to be wise in this absurd present?

Qoheleth foresees four possible situations, only one of which is positive; that is the advantage of wisdom over folly.

1. In v. 12b Qoheleth affirms that the one who comes after the king[32] cannot do anything new. The works of the future will not be any better. The results of present and future works are the same, as he has already said in 1:9. Is it worth it to give up part of one's life in work, if nothing will change in the future?

2. But in vv. 13 and 14, Qoheleth affirms with certainty that wisdom is better than folly. He agrees with the wisdom tradition that wisdom is like the light that overcomes the darkness. He even quotes a saying: "The wise have eyes in their head, but fools walk in darkness." It is better to understand the situation and to recognize failure and death, even though knowing the reality causes sorrow. To have eyes in one's head is to analyze all situations wisely. Fools don't know where they are going and cannot foresee their fall, because they are not aware of the dangers ahead. It is worth it, therefore, to be wise and not foolish.

3. But again, and at the same level as the foregoing affirmation, Qoheleth questions whether it is worth the effort to be wise. Before the end of v. 14, he invokes the wisdom tradition: "Yet I perceived. . . ." Here he refers to what other sages do not recognize: that death comes to both the wise and the foolish. Qoheleth is against the tradition that affirms long life for the

righteous, for the wise. To act wisely gives them no advantage over fools as far as death is concerned; they both die the same (v. 16). The only advantage of wisdom over foolishness, in Qoheleth's teaching, is that the wise know and understand, to their sorrow, the inhuman reality of their world.

4. Finally (2:16), he points out the worst: the deeds of the wise are forgotten. That the memory of the wise and their works is forgotten under the sun, that the wise and the fools are both forgotten by the coming generations (1:11), upsets him terribly. Qoheleth knows that he will die like everyone else, but what he cannot bear is that future generations will forget his works. He has invested too much effort and wisdom in his work, only to see it all pass into oblivion and not be continued by others. By forgetting what has been begun, each generation repeats the same past—without newness, without human fulfillment.

This is what is absurd (v. 15): that there will be no memory of his works, that he will die like the fools who did not act wisely. It is not historically important to remember the works of fools, but it is important to keep the memory of those who acted wisely. The lack of newness becomes a problem when peoples lose their historical memory, because they lose the path that would lead them to a new and longed-for future.

Qoheleth then raises a bitter cry, uncharacteristic of a sage: "So I hated life" (v. 17). The wise never hate life; on the contrary, wisdom leads to life. But having seen terrible things he cannot suppress his frustration, and like that other wise man, Job (Job 3:3), he hates life. This is a cry of despair in a situation of closed horizons. He hates life, not because he doesn't want to live but because he wants to live in satisfaction. But the present closes off his path; the events of his history deny him fulfillment as a living being who takes pleasure in his creative works. The deeds that are done under the sun become a heavy, unbearable burden.

He ends this section with his well-known verdict on reality: it is all an absurdity, a chasing of wind, a frustration, a waste of time.

The Frustration of Not Enjoying the Fruit of One's Labor (2:18-23)

> [18]*I hated all my toil in which I had toiled under the sun, seeing that I must leave it to those who come after me* [19]*—and who knows whether they will be wise or foolish? Yet they will be master of all for which I toiled and used my wisdom under the sun. This also is vanity.* [20]*So I turned and gave my heart up to despair concerning all the toil of my labors under the sun,* [21]*because sometimes one who has toiled with wisdom and knowledge and skill must leave all to be enjoyed by another who did not toil for it. This also is vanity and a great evil.* [22]*What do mortals get from all the toil and strain with which they toil under the sun?* [23]*For all their days are full of pain, and their work is a vexation; even at night their minds do not rest. This also is vanity.*

Frustration comes to a climax in this section. The key words in the text show the depth of the self's anger, despair, and frustration. Here the self does not have the dignity or the authority one expects of a sovereign, as it has in 2:3-10. The circumstances of his world have closed in on him until he explodes with indignation. We do not even hear the words of a wise self in the classic tradition: spoken with prudence, equanimity, and restraint. Rather we hear the desperate voice of one who is struggling against the injustice that occurs under the sun, powerless to intervene effectively and change its course.

In this fragment he emphasizes the reasons for despair by repetition: enslaving, troublesome toil, and the fact that another, who does not work, takes possession of the product of labor (vv. 18, 19, 21). What is worse, he does not know who will inherit the results of so much effort, whether they will be wise or foolish (v. 19). Each of these three frustrations is described with the phrase, "This also is vanity" (*gam zeh hebel*) (vv. 19, 21, 23). To the second he adds, "and a great evil" (v. 21).

The underlying problem of vv. 18-23 is that another will be

master of the work he did with so much effort and wisdom. The Hebrew word ʿamal (enslaving toil) appears eleven times in these six verses. He is talking about difficult, heavy work that requires a lot of effort and knowledge. The text repeats three times that another will be master of that work. In v. 18 we read: "I must leave it to those who come after me;" in v. 19, "they will be master of all for which I toiled"; and in v. 21, "must leave all to be enjoyed by another who did not toil for it."

Behind the text are anger and helplessness. Not only because the work itself is enslaving and troublesome, but especially because Qoheleth cannot enjoy its fruit, since another will be master of it. Thus, everyday life becomes a vexation for the worker, and the nights are filled with anguished, restless reflections.

Here we must ask again about the identity of the narrator and about "the ones who come after him" to take mastery of his goods. We know that he has presented himself as king of Israel in Jerusalem (1:12). We said that this is an ancient literary tradition that enables the speaker to present some teachings. Indeed, in 1:16-2:11 he acts as a king; but in 2:12-26 his experience as a wise, party-going, and hard-working king merges with the experience of other sectors besides royalty. His identity is visible from several angles. First, from the angle of the wealthy who because of their ambition are only interested in accumulating wealth, who do not enjoy either their days or their nights, and who suffer because they will have to pass it on to an undeserving other. If we think of the narrator as a king, this is a strong criticism of Solomon's ambition. The point would then be that riches do not bring happiness; his attachment to riches shows his selfishness, so much so that it pains him to think of another inheriting his goods undeservedly.

But this is not the point, if his basic purpose in referring back through the centuries to Solomon is to criticize the rich aristocracy of his own time, both in Palestine and in Egypt. Attachment to wealth and concern for the future of one's property were characteristic of the Hellenistic society.[33] Qoheleth criticizes this attitude in 4:8 and 6:3-6.

Another angle might be criticism of the economic policies of the Ptolemies: as rulers of the provinces they could appropriate the property of others whenever they wanted, under any pretext, and give it to their Greek officials or other subjects.[34] The insecurity of wealth was real. So Qoheleth's conclusion makes sense. It is not worth it, it is a waste of time or a chasing of wind, to work with so much effort and wisdom if someone else is going to come and take over the product of one's toil.

Finally, the criticism could be extended to speak for all workers who cannot enjoy the fruits of their labor because of exploitation. Qoheleth has seen oppression under the sun (4:1ff.) In vv. 18-23 he seems to represent all the workers of his land, whose work suffers the same fate. The Papyri of Zeno tell of a Palestinian peasant who bitterly complains to Zeno that the wages promised him are often withheld.[35] Many modern Latin American sayings reflect the same abuse: "The worst dish is the one you cook but can't eat"; "No one knows who they're working for"; "You do the work and someone else gets the credit"; "You get the rabbit in the field, and someone else gets it on a plate."

So then, it is frustrating to "work up a sweat for nothing"; it is a great evil, a chasing of wind, an affliction of the spirit.

There Is Nothing Better Than to Enjoy Life and the Fruit of One's Labor (2:24-26)

> [24]*There is nothing better for mortals than to eat and drink, and find enjoyment in their toil. This also, I saw, is from the hand of God;* [25]*for apart from him who can eat or who can have enjoyment?* [26]*For to the one who pleases him God gives wisdom and knowledge and joy; but to the sinner he gives the work of gathering and heaping, only to give to one who pleases God. This also is vanity and a chasing after wind.*

Here at last there is something positive in the midst of frustration. We first glimpsed this enjoyment of life in 2:10, with the experience of pleasure in toil.

Verses 24-26 are the conclusion to his analysis of reality. In 1:13, the self set out to perform the painful task God has given him, to know and understand what happens in history; he set out with wisdom and knowledge to discover the good (*tob*), or the good-and-beautiful, in what mortals do (2:3). He followed the paths of wisdom, pleasure, and work, always with wisdom. These paths led him to a single result: it is all absurd, useless, like shepherding the wind. He did not find the human fulfillment he was seeking, nor did he see any future possibility of finding it. But even in the midst of the total frustration he has found something, which he describes with the refrain, "There is nothing better for mortals than. . . ." This judgment about the possibility of a better quality of life now frees the self, and the reader, from suicide.

The refrain is repeated six times,[36] almost with a rising intensity, until it reaches its most complete expression in 9:7-10.

The happy experience of eating, drinking, and enjoying one's work, is the simple advice offered by the self in the face of the frustration caused by reality. Qoheleth does not propose to evade or justify that frustration, nor does he suggest waiting in bitter resignation for death to come. He proposes affirming real life. If the cosmos and historical events do not take subjects into account with all their consciousness and subjectivity, the subjects will have to make human beings the goal of their attitudes and practices. This is how we must interpret 2:25.[37]

A joyful meal and work that can be enjoyed in itself as well as its fruits lead to human self-fulfillment. Faced with a machine that he believes will not allow interference, Qoheleth proposes a contrary attitude. He offers a different rhythm, a human rhythm in which one feels the pulsation of life. In the particular situation of that century one could only follow that rhythm in everyday life, amid the material things and the subjectivity that bring joy to the mind and nourish the body, so that human beings can feel their humanity.

In order to freely affirm real life, Qoheleth has reached the conclusion that this experience comes from God. It is a gift of God. The phrase "this too" is the counterpart of the same phrase (*gam zeh*) that appears three times in 2:19, 21, and 23. But there the predicate is "absurdity," "vanity"; here it is a gift of God.

In 2:26 we find a contradiction with the thought expressed in v. 21. In that verse one person works with zeal and wisdom, and someone else enjoys the fruit. Here, in v. 26, Qoheleth follows the line of traditional wisdom. The one who pleases God receives wisdom and knowledge and joy; God gives the sinner[38] the work of gathering and heaping, in order to give it to one who pleases God.

To find a coherent interpretation of this verse, one might read in it that a person so anxious for riches (the one who gathers and heaps), like the prototypes mentioned in 2:6-9 and 4:8, is not pleasing to God. The consequences of that one's acts are vexation and insomnia (2:23). On the other hand, the one who pleases God is the one who behaves with wisdom and knowledge and is therefore able to enjoy life. The virtues of wisdom, knowledge, and enjoyment are the gift of God. Thus, riches, as a source of enjoyment, become secondary.

SECTION II

Facing the Present with Trust
in God's Grace (3:1-6:12)

After the negative climax of the preceding section (2:18-23) and the briefly glimpsed possibility of resisting total frustration (2:24-26), in this section (3:1-6:12) Qoheleth steps forward with an invitation to take a new look at the frustrating events under the sun. While he sees a dehumanizing reality in his world, his attitude of frustration and helplessness has also contributed to his own dehumanization. This combination of the real situation and a subjective attitude of total frustration has not only embittered his existence but also paralyzed any action he might want to take—because he knows in his mind that "what is crooked cannot be made straight" (1:15), and that he cannot change the way the sun rises and sets (1:5).

But by believing that there is a time and a season for everything—and that God knows the course of history—Qoheleth is able to face the difficult present with maturity, trusting in God's grace. In this section he establishes the importance of recognizing one's human limitations. Not in order to minimize the limitations but to permit fulfillment as a human being. To recognize our limitations is to recognize our humanity. When we accept the limited reach of our own actions, we are better able to take on the present with maturity, effectiveness, solidarity, and humaneness. This is where the fear of God comes in, in the sage's exhortation to respect the distance between God in heaven and human beings on earth (5:2 [Heb. 5:1]).

Qoheleth 3:16-6:9 repeats, in greater detail, the situations of total frustration that the narrator has described earlier. Now he

steps away from his own experience, to examine other people's
frustration with injustice, the love of riches, envy, and the inability to enjoy life. He observes that society has been turned upside
down, with wickedness in the very courts that were set up to do
justice (3:16). Frustration is aggravated by the helplessness that
we feel in situations that seem immutable. That is why we need
to know that God is aware of the situation, that God is directing
history—sometimes in ways that the human mind cannot grasp.
To fear God is to recognize the limits of our humanity. It
means to trust God; it does not mean "don't be afraid" in this
frustration-filled present. God's grace is above the laws of the
universe and the dehumanizing system. Therefore we must do
the best we can and live with intensity those gratifying moments
that cheer the body and the mind. This message is repeated at
the end of each of the five units in this section. The situation is
frustrating; it is important to know our limits (a human being is
not God); and we must enjoy the good, humanizing things of
everyday life. That helps people avoid being overwhelmed by
the present. If it is impossible to interfere with unjust social
structures now, then we must try now to enjoy such humanizing moments as eating, drinking, enjoying the fruit of toil. He is
advising us to feel the breeze, and to take time to watch the sunset. If it is impossible to confront the Ptolemaic empire now, at
least one can avoid being overwhelmed by it. There is a time for
everything.

Verses 10-12 of chapter 6 end the section with a renewed
emphasis on human limitations and on the uselessness of disput-
ing with God.

THE TIMES OF HISTORY (3:1-15)

Two basic ideas are developed in this first unit: that there is a
time for everything, and that no one can comprehend the works
of God. The key word is time; it appears twenty-eight times and
refers to a given possibility of each time.[1]

There Is a Time for Everything (3:1-9)

> *3¹ For everything there is a season, and a time for every*
> *matter under heaven:*
> ² *a time to be born, and a time to die;*
> *a time to plant, and a time to pluck up what is*
> *planted;*
> ³ *a time to kill, and a time to heal;*
> *a time to break down, and a time to build up;*
> ⁴ *a time to weep, and a time to laugh;*
> *a time to mourn, and a time to dance;*
> ⁵ *a time to throw away stones, and a time to gather*
> *stones together;*
> *a time to embrace, and a time to refrain from*
> *embracing;*
> ⁶ *a time to seek, and a time to lose;*
> *a time to keep, and a time to throw away;*
> ⁷ *a time to tear, and a time to sew;*
> *a time to keep silence, and a time to speak;*
> ⁸ *a time to love, and a time to hate;*
> *a time for war, and a time for peace.*
> ⁹*What gain have the workers from their toil?*

The first and last phrases (3:1 and 3:9) frame a beautiful poem constructed of fourteen phrases in antithetical pairs (7 × 2). The word "time" (ʿet) appears twice in each phrase, for a total of twenty-eight.

These are impersonal phrases; neither the subject who acts nor the object who experiences the action is mentioned. The impersonal expression "there is" (a time to . . .) is also implicit in each phrase. This listing of the phrases in a lyrical meditation creates a great impact on the reader.[2] The absence of subjects also adds meaning to the text. That is, in extreme cases like birth and death, one must accept the impossibility of human intervention. The whole poem is an invitation to embrace God's grace and to have faith that situations will change. There is wisdom in recognizing that there are good and bad situations in life. In the bad situations one must have faith that there will be good ones, and one must make use of the moments that bring joy to one's life in the midst of negativity. One must also make use of the good situations, and enjoy them as much as possible, knowing that there will be bad times and that death will come in its season.

Two Hebrew words for "time" appear in 3:1; both represent specific points rather than continuity.[3] The Greek Bible (Septuagint, LXX) renders *zman* and *'et* respectively as *chronos* and *kairos*. The two Hebrew words have almost the same meaning, although one might say that *zman* (an Aramaic term of Persian origin) means a specific time and *'et* an appropriate time.[4] Their conjunction here as parallel terms reinforces the sense of an appropriate, opportune time.

To affirm that there is a time for every event, matter, or human activity implies that there is no cause for alarm, that everything is in God's hands.[5] God is the implied subject of the present actions in the poem.

The meaning of time (*'et*) in vv. 2-8 does not suggest temporal moments, but rather refers to particular situations or occasions, that is, to the concrete structure of a given situation.[6] These verses embrace the totality of human existence, describing it in antitheses like birth and death, love and hate, peace and war. It is not by chance that there are fourteen pairs, two times seven; in Hebrew that number signifies fullness or totality.

In v. 2 to be born and to die, to plant and pluck up represent the beginning and end of human, plant, or animal life. The text moves from human existence to labor, to the hard work of agriculture, which may be wasted for a variety of reasons (cf. Isaiah 5:1-6).[7]

The events of v. 3 are placed chiastically in relation to v. 2; here the negative comes first. The antithesis of killing is preserving life, healing.

The activities of breaking down and building up are not precisely described; they may refer to human actions in relation to things, while v. 3 refers to positive or negative activities in relation to other human beings.

The two pairs in v. 4 correspond to emotional states; mourning refers to sorrow, and dancing to celebration.

The act of throwing away stones and gathering them together (v. 5) has provoked some discussion. Taken literally, it might mean a trivial action and counteraction. In the *Midrash Qohelet Rabbah,* the two acts are interpreted as having, and abstaining from, sexual relations.[8] The second part refers to a loving relationship as embracing, and not embracing. If one accepts this interpretation, it points to a direct connection between the two pairs in v. 5. But this interpretation is found only in the one *Midrash.*

To seek and to lose (v. 6) may refer to property.[9] These are common events in the commercial activity of Qoheleth's time.

In v. 7, tearing probably means tearing one's clothing, a sign of mourning or sorrow, "a sign of the wounded dignity of a person."[10] Sewing is then a metaphor for the opposite, a time to repair the sign of sorrow.

The second pair in v. 7 suggests that there are propitious occasions for speaking and keeping silence. Job's friends Eliphaz, Bildad, and Zophar tore their clothing and kept silence for seven days and seven nights as a sign of solidarity with Job (Job 2:13). Qoheleth is referring to the importance of knowing when to speak and when to keep silence in a situation of repression (8:4, 6; 10:20).

The last two pairs, in v. 8, are related chiastically to each other (love and war, hate and peace), and also to the initial pair in v. 2 (birth and death, war and peace).

The first pair in v. 8 refers to the basic attitudes of human relationships, love and hate; the second to the structural situation of global society, as shown in war or peace (*shalom*). *Shalom* means not only the absence of war but a situation of community well-being. That the poem ends with the term *shalom* is significant. Although everything is vanity for Qoheleth, he offers a spark of hope by opening his lyrical discourse with birth, and ending with *shalom.*[11]

Verse 9 returns to the rhetorical question of 1:3 and 2:22, which will be repeated in 5:15: "What gain have the workers from their toil?" The question has the same meaning in each occurrence, with minimal variations in the Hebrew text. Here in v. 9 the human being as subject (*ʾadam*) is replaced by the one who does, the one who works (*haʿoseh*); this is intensified by hard work, toil (*ʿamal*) at the end of the verse. The negation is implicit in the question itself: there is nothing to be gained by so much toil. The negation is not intended to discourage the one who works. The poem in vv. 2-8 answers the question in order to encourage the subject. It means: do not let the oppressive present overwhelm you, nor be concerned for the future. There is a propitious occasion for every situation. There is no point in wasting one's life; one should not always be disappointed or frustrated; God is in control of events under the sun.

This meaning is echoed by Jesus' words in the Gospel of Matthew: "Look at the birds of the air; they neither sow nor reap. . . . And why do you worry about clothing? Consider the lilies of the field, how they grow; they neither toil nor spin . . ." (Matthew 6:26-29).

Qoheleth's recommendation is to accept life as a gift of God and to make use of its gratifying moments. The important thing in these discouraging situations is to discern the times and not to live against the times.[12]

This does not mean folding one's arms and waiting for the good time to come. The poem simply suggests the importance of knowing consciously that at given historical moments one builds, sows, loves, and seeks peace, even in times of war, hate, uprooting, and destruction. This is much harder to do than to build, sow, love, and seek peace in times of peace, love, sowing, and building.

If we know that sometimes "you can't make the dawn come by getting up early," then we can sleep a little longer and not be totally frustrated when things come out wrong.

Celso Coropa, a character in Carlos Salazar Herrera's story "The Mountain," doesn't always enjoy life. "Sometimes I don't like living," he sighed when "he picked up a sunbeam in the palm of his hand," because "in front of him there was a torture of roots and vines." But then he said, "And sometimes I do," because "amid the torture of roots and vines there was a flower."[13]

Grace is the flower; that alone makes life worth living, struggling for, and enjoying.

The Work of God Is a Mystery (3:10-15)

[10]I have seen the business that God has given to everyone to be busy with. [11]He has made everything suitable for its time; moreover he has put a sense of past and future into their minds, yet they cannot find out what God has done from the beginning to the end. [12]I know that there is nothing better for them than to be happy and enjoy themselves as long as they live; [13]moreover, it is God's gift that all should eat and drink and take pleasure in all their toil. [14]I know that whatever God does endures forever; nothing can be added to it, nor anything taken from it; God has done this, so that all should stand in awe before him. [15]That which is, already has been; that which is to be, already is; and God seeks out what has gone by.

In this fragment Qoheleth follows the same purpose as before, only now more directly. The understanding of human beings is limited. We cannot understand all the events of history (v. 11); therefore it is better to overcome frustration. To do so we should enjoy and do the best we can while we live. We should accept God's gift of enjoying whatever in the present makes us feel like living beings, not like objects: eating, drinking, and feeling joy. All human beings have a right to enjoy the benefits of their labor, as gifts of God.

It is dehumanizing to try to do everything without looking for the opportune moment. Human beings are not God; they cannot make the crooked straight or change things when the time is not right. The last two verses (14-15) emphasize trust, by explaining that God has everything under control; God has not forgotten God's creatures. To fear God (NRSV: "stand in awe before him") does not mean to be afraid of God; rather, by recognizing their own limitations, human beings cease to fear the oppressive present, the uncertain future, and the forgotten past. God knows the past, the present, and the future. God's creation and God's times are everlasting. By doing the best we can and enjoying life, we can live under the grace of God in times of total frustration.

Verse 10 repeats Qoheleth's idea from 1:13b: God gives human beings a business to occupy them.[14] While in 1:13 he describes it as a unhappy business (*ra*ᶜ), here he withholds judgment. As in 1:13, this work or occupation is connected with knowing and understanding what is happening. In 1:13 knowledge led to suffering, because of his feeling of helplessness over the unjust things that happen. Here in 3:10 it does not. Rather, v. 11 explains that human beings cannot understand events or reality in their totality. He understands that God is the creator of all things, and that all things are beautifully made. Human beings can understand perfectly, because God gave them the ability to perceive events as a whole, or the mystery of the hidden.

Forever (*ᶜolam*) can have several meanings: unlimited duration; the distant, the hidden; or the sum of everything real, that is, all the events of history.[15] Thus human beings have the potential to understand more than what is given. But in spite of this, Qoheleth finds it impossible to understand all of reality; the work of God, from the beginning to the end, surprises him and overwhelms his expectations. In 8:17 he says again that despite having fully seen (*raʾah*) God's work, he cannot comprehend it. As a wise man, he can know God's work but not explain it.

Thus, recognizing his inability to understand, he must look for happiness in the material world of everyday intimacy. This is a better, more human way to be happy in times of despair; it is also the best way to resist frustration.

"Nothing can be added to it, nor anything taken from it" (v. 14) is an ancient formula.[16] The expression "fear of God" emphasizes the difference between God and human beings; it means respecting the sacred, an indisputable and inscrutable power.[17] It points to the need to accept the boundaries of the human condition, so as not to live in frustration with the impossibility of changing the world or explaining all of history, from the beginning to the end.

In 3:15 he returns to a theme from the first part (1:9), holding together the past, present, and future. But here he does not explicitly deny the possibility of newness, as in 1:9. Read from the logic of chapter 3, this verse may even have the opposite meaning; it alleviates the frustration. In the first part the absence of newness, the monotony of the times, contributed to a total disappointment with everything that happens under the sun. Here newness is not explicitly denied; the meaning of the text may turn on the security that comes from understanding that what was before, what is now, and what is to be are not unknown or uncertain. They are in God's realm, because God is the subject of the times (3:1-8).

The last part of v. 15 is obscure. It may be a popular saying that the readers of the text would have understood.[18] Other translations read: "God will seek out what has disappeared," "God reaches out to what is pursued." Graham Ogden suggests, "God requires that it be pursued," or "God requires us to pursue it."[19]

INJUSTICE AND SOLIDARITY (3:16-4:16)

In this second unit of the section, Qoheleth goes back to being an eyewitness who sees, fully, the reality that happens under the sun. He sees the reality of injustice (3:16), violence (4:1), envy of another (4:4), the absurdity of solitary individuals without sons or brothers (4:7), and a multitude following a poor but wise youth who replaces the king, although later they will also be disappointed in him (4:10-16). He also sees, as he did earlier in the book, that for human beings there is nothing better than taking enjoyment in work.

After observing this reality, he reflects consciously ("I said in my heart") on the fact that death makes beasts and humans equal (3:18-21), and on the dead and the unborn, who do not have the misfortune of seeing this violence against the oppressed and the lack of solidarity (4:2-3). The whole unit describes this painful reality and classifies it as absurd. The word "vanity" (*hebel*) appears five times in this unit (3:19; 4:4, 7, 8, 15); to the last Qoheleth adds "and a chasing after wind."

God Has Appointed a Time for Justice (3:16-22)

> [16]*Moreover I saw under the sun that in the place of justice, wickedness was there, and in the place of righteousness, wickedness was there as well.* [17]*I said in my heart, God will judge the righteous and the wicked, for he has appointed a time for every matter, and for every work.* [18]*I said in my heart with regard to human beings that God is testing them to show that they are but animals.* [19]*For the fate of humans and the fate of animals is the same; as one dies, so dies the other. They all have the same breath, and humans have no advantage over the animals; for all is vanity.* [20]*All go to one place; all are from the dust, and all turn to dust again.* [21]*Who knows whether the human spirit goes upward and the spirit of animals goes downward to the earth?* [22]*So I saw that there is nothing better than that all should enjoy their work, for that is their lot; who can bring them to see what will be after them?*

Qoheleth sees society as inverted. In the courts, which were supposedly established to do justice, the judges are wicked; they favor the guilty. The victims do not receive justice (3:16). This verdict should not be understood as a mere echo of the prophets (cf. Isaiah 5:6); Qoheleth is analyzing his own world. Robert Michaud sees it as a picture of the Ptolemaic regime: "The regime of the Ptolemies, greedy for money, is especially oppressive to the poor population of Judea. Qoheleth could have cited many cases of arbitrary abuse. In cities that refused to pay their exorbitant taxes, the royal tax collector had the power to condemn magistrates to death."[20]

He answers the problem in 3:17,[21] with a well-known affirmation.[22] We must interpret his meaning in the context of this whole section (3:1-6:12). Again he affirms his faith that there is a right time for every event and a place for every action. The poem in 3:1-8 is now extended to include the dimension of justice and injustice. The emphasis is on the coming time (*'et*) of justice, because God will act in a different way from what Qoheleth observes. God's justice will favor the innocent victims. In Qoheleth's view, God cannot remain indifferent; God must put things in order, "make the crooked straight." God's justice will appear in events under the sun, not on the other side of death. In Qoheleth's time there was not yet a concept of resurrection or of life beyond death.

Qoheleth's second reflection, in v. 3:18, is surprising.[23] It begins with the same phrase as 3:17: "I said in my heart . . . ," but then takes off in a different direction. Verse 17 was about God's action for justice at the right time. Verse 18 is about created reality, in which God makes human beings[24] recognize that they are like beasts. These are two separate reflections on the reality of the unjust society described in 3:16.

It is hard to extract their meaning. Perhaps the author was trying to establish the difference between the actions of humans and those of God. Qoheleth feels helpless in the face of the reality described in 3:16; he believes his affirmation in 3:17, but it is important to him to reflect on the fragility and impermanence[25] of the human condition, which is like that of beasts. Human beings have no need to show their superiority, already affirmed by tradition (cf. Psalm 8:4-5), or to enter into competition with animals. Death introduces equality between humans and animals. Death also establishes the difference between all created life and God.

Meanwhile the Greek ideology, dispersed throughout the provinces, was placing an immense and optimistic trust in human reason and boasting of its unlimited capabilities.[26] Qoheleth seems to be putting human beings in their place and thereby conveying a two-sided message. He is reminding his own people that human beings are finite, in order to raise their morale and diminish their frustration with their inability to change things and open up the horizons. And he is reminding the Greeks, who see themselves as gods, of their human condition; they are like animals. Human beings are not immortal.[27]

Verse 20 invokes Genesis 2:7 and 3:19. The idea that humans are made of dust and will return to dust when they die is common in the Hebrew tradition.[28] The phrase "all go to one place" refers to *sheol* (cf. 9:10), the dwelling place of death, the place of shadows. Ogden points out that this verse uses the key words of 1:7: "all," "place," "go," and "return."

In v. 21 Qoheleth pursues his point that human beings are not superior to animals. Since there is no way to know what will happen after death, one cannot affirm that the human spirit goes upward and the spirit of animals goes downward to the earth.[29] "Downward to the earth" is a way of saying far from God. When he speaks of death in 12:7, Qoheleth says again that the creature returns to the earth as dust and the spirit returns to God; that is, the elements return to their original source.[30] His affirmation that the spirit returns to God (3:20) seems to contradict 3:21. But in 3:21 he is trying to establish a difference between human beings and animals even after death, since no one knows whether there will be a difference in the end.

That is why, in 3:21, he raises a rhetorical question that demands a negative answer. No one can bring him to see what will happen after his death. As a conclusion to his two reflections on 3:16, Qoheleth repeats the answer that he proposed in the preceding section. Faced with helplessness, frustration, and bitterness against the unjust order of his society, and unable to foresee the future (3:21, 22b), human beings can only find humanization in their enjoyment of work. That is their reward, their portion (*heleq*).[31] They have a right to it. The affirmation of 3:17, that God will judge rightly, enables Qoheleth to step forward and feel the present in a more humanizing way—in spite of death, or rather, because he knows that death takes away the difference between humans and beasts, placing them on the same level.

Solidarity in the Face of Violence, Envy, and Loneliness (4:1-12)

Qoheleth goes on describing absurd and painful situations in his world. These situations reveal the lack of solidarity among human beings. Therefore, modestly, he proposes solidarity as a way of combating the avaricious and meaningless spirit of his society. In an anti-human reality where people are ignored as subjects, Qoheleth proposes that they unite. Thus, to his advice about eating, drinking, and enjoying their work to relieve the frustration of the present, he now adds a recommendation about unity and solidarity among humans (4:12b).

This is reflected in the structure that Ogden proposes for 4:1-12.[32] Here we find three observations with their respective conclusions, followed by three conditional clauses in 4:10-12a. The observations reveal the situation of oppression, bad relationships in work, and the loneliness of the avaricious worker. The conditional clauses emphasize the value of solidarity. The structure can be schematized as follows:

4:1	Again I saw	Observation A
4:3	Better than both is	Conclusion A
4:4	Then I saw that	Observation B
4:6	Better is a handful	Conclusion B
4:7	Again I saw	Observation C
4:9	Two are better than one	Conclusion C
4:10	For if they fall	Condition 1
4:11	Again, if two lie together	Condition 2
4:12a	And though one might prevail	Condition 3
4:12b	A threefold cord	Final conclusion

The Tears of the Oppressed (4:1-3)

4¹Again I saw all the oppressions that are practiced under the sun. Look, the tears of the oppressed—with no one to comfort them! On the side of their oppressors there was power—with no one to comfort them. ²And I thought the dead, who have already died, more fortunate than the living, who are still alive; ³but better than both is the one who has not yet been, and has not seen the evil deeds that are done under the sun.

Verse 1 is a radical critique of the oppressive society, which does not hear the cries of its victims. The root word for oppression is repeated three times. The Hebrew term used here for oppression (ʿashaq) is very strong, implying violence. This text, like 3:16, is a prophetic denunciation of oppression and injustice.

Twice Qoheleth says that the oppressed have no one to comfort them. He is invoking the prophetic, wisdom, and psalmic traditions which affirm that God hears the cry of the oppressed. Thus he criticizes the whole society for its lack of solidarity.

The Hebrew word "to console" is not merely about spiritual consolation. It is of juridical origin and also connotes rehabilitation:³³ "As in the New Testament the Paraclete both consoles and gives strength to confront the persecutions and distortions of history, so also the Old Testament 'consoler' is actively allied with the oppressed."³⁴

In Qoheleth's society there is no reliable system of justice (3:16; 5:8 [Heb. 5:7]); apparently the motto is "save your own skin." The invertedness reflected in 3:16 is described candidly here: the oppressors have power on their side, so there is no possibility of liberation.

The readers know that situation. Michaud describes it bluntly: "The wealthy in the ruling class exploit the rural population and the urban artisans. They have rights over the people and their work, either directly through slavery, or indirectly through the economic monopoly they wield."³⁵

So great is Qoheleth's sorrow over his society that, apparently in his rage, he can think of nothing but to congratulate the dead—and even more, those who have not been born. Not because he is contemplating suicide or something like it but because they do not see what he sees. The unborn are the happiest of all, because they have no idea what it is to live in an unjust society (v. 3). This kind of life is worse than death.

Unbridled Competition (4:4-6)

>⁴*Then I saw that all toil and all skill in work come from one person's envy of another. This also is vanity and a chasing after wind.*
>⁵*Fools fold their hands*
>   *and consume their own flesh.*
>⁶*Better is a handful with quiet*
>   *than two handfuls with toil,*
>   *and a chasing after wind.*

These verses point to the problem of rivalry. A society of "save your own skin" is a society of "all against all." Qoheleth is not criticizing work in itself but rather the frenzied pursuit of success. He observes that people in his society tend to work without restraint, always trying to be better than others.[36] This attitude provokes envy among their fellow workers and leads to no good. Qoheleth classifies it as absurd (*hebel*) and deceptive.

Qoheleth is obviously describing the society of the third century B.C.E. "A competitive, unbridled zeal reigned in the time of the Ptolemies, in the economic system and in the state administration. To see this, one needs only to look at the importance assigned to the commercial center of the Rock . . . and the feverish activity of the financiers and courtesans under Ptolemy II."[37] It could also be seen in Palestine, in "the ascension of Joseph of the Tobiads during the reign of Ptolemy III, the eccentricities of his son Hyrcanus in the court of Ptolemy IV."[38]

From the observation in v. 4, Qoheleth moves to the corresponding conclusion in vv. 5-6. He quotes two proverbs familiar to his listeners. The first, in a negative tone, may refer to idlers: to fold one's hands means not to work. Here Qoheleth may be referring to the classic wisdom tradition against laziness.[39] The consequence of laziness is starvation, that is, to consume one's own flesh.[40] The narrator is using a grotesque metaphor for self-destructiveness, says C.-L. Seow: it is self-cannibalism.[41] To Gianfranco Ravasi, the proverb represents the lazy one who spends his time watching others work, using up his life "without having or doing anything that would make his existence vital and enjoyable."[42]

The second proverb is Qoheleth's own proposal, as absurd and frustrating as the conclusions he reaches after observing his world (2:24; 3:12, 13, 22). This time he proposes to work—but with tranquillity, without destructive competitiveness, even though the fruits are less than one would get from the frenzied, restless work that afflicts the spirit because it is a chasing after wind (4:6).

On Biting Off More Than One Can Chew (4:7-8)

> [7]*Again, I saw vanity under the sun:* [8]*the case of solitary individuals, without sons or brothers; yet there is no end to all their toil, and their eyes are never satisfied with riches. "For whom am I toiling," they ask, "and depriving myself of pleasure?" This also is vanity and an unhappy business.*

Again Qoheleth is analyzing the events of his history. He continues the theme of enslaving, unhappy labor, the goal of which is the accumulation of wealth and not human fulfillment. There is no rest for workaholics. They are like a machine that will not allow interference, that is never satisfied (cf. 1:4-11). The worst of it is that there is no objective or purpose in unbridled work. The subjects of work are alone; they have no companions,[43] children, or family members to enjoy the fruit of their work. They do not enjoy it themselves, because of their constant busyness and their anxiety to accumulate riches. They do not even stop to ask what is happening to the fruit of their work, or for whose sake they are depriving themselves of pleasure. They are completely alienated. The text frames this situation at the beginning and end of vv. 7-8 with the word *hebel*, "absurd," "vanity." At the end of v. 8 it adds that this is an "unhappy business."

In Unity There Is Strength (4:9-12)

>⁹*Two are better than one, because they have a good reward for their toil. ¹⁰For if they fall, one will lift up the other; but woe to one who is alone and falls and does not have another to help. ¹¹Again, if two lie together, they keep warm; but how can one keep warm alone? ¹²And though one might prevail against another, two will withstand one. A threefold cord is not quickly broken.*

The final conclusion comes from the previous observation (vv. 7-8). But it is not only the conclusion to vv. 7-8; it applies to the whole series (4:1-8). It is about the advantages of solidarity in a society where absurdity reigns. In order to withstand and overcome a society dominated by the logic of "save your own skin" and "all against all," it is not advisable to be alone; one must seek the company of others—in this case, not only in order to eat and drink and share the enjoyment of work but to get a better wage, pull each other up, ward off the cold,[44] and face an enemy attack. Similar references are found in *Gilgamesh* and in the heroes of the *Iliad*.

The last proverb (v. 12b) summarizes this advice: "A threefold cord is not quickly broken."[45]

On the Wisdom of Taking Advice (4:13-16)

>¹³*Better is a poor but wise youth than an old but foolish king, who will no longer take advice. ¹⁴One can indeed come out of prison to reign, even though born poor in the kingdom. ¹⁵I saw all the living who, moving about under the sun, follow that youth who replaced the king; ¹⁶there was no end to all those people whom he led. Yet those who come later will not rejoice in him. Surely this also is vanity and a chasing after wind.*

Verses 13 and 14 are self-explanatory. Qoheleth is emphasizing the importance of seeking wisdom, which is worth more than riches or power. This valuation is characteristic of the wisdom tradition. The wise one is the one disposed to listen to advice (Proverbs 12:15; 13:10). But Qoheleth is also pointing out that the old are not always wise, nor the young always foolish, as the wisdom tradition usually supposes. In ancient times, youth and poverty were less desirable than maturity and royalty. Youth, it was believed, was more vulnerable to sensuality; poverty was the fruit of laziness.[46] Guided by experience, Qoheleth shows that the poor youth, if he is wise, is worth more than the old king who will not take advice.

In v. 14 he repeats the same point, referring to the handicaps of the successor: he is not only poor but has been in prison. Even so, by his wisdom he surpasses the old, rich king, who came to power as a rich man and had never been in prison. This verse has provoked some debate. While some commentators seek to identify the poor man with a historical figure, others simply interpret it as a universal declaration: to be able to take advice is better than being rich and old. Several commentators see the son as a reference to Joseph, the son of Jacob, who also was poor, came out of prison, and was an advisor to Pharaoh.[47] Ogden believes that Qoheleth was thinking of Joseph (who came out of prison) and of David (who was poor) as representative examples.[48] Others believe he was referring to the Ptolemies or the Seleucid kings.[49]

Still others, linking this to the following verse, see it as a story in which a young man supplants a king; whether by revolution or a change of dynasty, the king is dethroned and the young leader of the conspiracy, wise and poor, comes out of jail to take power.[50] With Vílchez, I believe this is a paradigm common in many power struggles rather than a specific historical event.[51]

The next two verses (15-16) can be interpreted in different ways. In one, we see Qoheleth's viewpoint as described earlier, that is, his reproach to the generations who forget the good works of those who do good (cf. 1:11; 2:16; 8:10). This interpretation fits with Qoheleth's other anecdote (9:14-15), about a wise youth who delivered the city but was later forgotten.

Another interpretation of 4:15-16 is based on Qoheleth's

cyclical view of the world. In this view he is predicting the dissatisfaction of future generations with the ruler who now is admired by the multitude. Perhaps he is foreseeing the failure of all power structures. The poor, wise youth comes to power and ceases to be poor; with passing time he becomes old and his wisdom turns to foolishness, because power and wisdom contradict each other in practice. In this case, the multitude is right to be dissatisfied.

THE MYSTERY OF GOD
(5:1-7 [Heb. 4:17-5:6])[52]

5¹Guard your steps when you go to the house of God; to draw near to listen is better than the sacrifice offered by fools; for they do not know how to keep from doing evil. ²Never be rash with your mouth, nor let your heart be quick to utter a word before God, for God is in heaven, and you upon earth; therefore let your words be few.

³For dreams come with many cares, and a fool's voice with many words.

⁴When you make a vow to God, do not delay fulfilling it; for he has no pleasure in fools. Fulfill what you vow. ⁵It is better that you should not vow than that you should vow and not fulfill it. ⁶Do not let your mouth lead you into sin, and do not say before the messenger that it was a mistake; why should God be angry at your words, and destroy the work of your hands?

⁷With many dreams come vanities and a multitude of words; but fear God!

The attitude and behavior that Qoheleth recommends for the relationship between humans and God are distilled in these seven verses. God is named six times in these verses, and forty times in the whole book. This part comes as a surprise to the reader who, until this part of the book, has been hearing affirmations that seem a bit heterodox in the context of his time.

One expects to read something different, more provocative, about God. Instead, the material in 5:1-7 [Heb. 4:17-5:6] is traditional. Qoheleth is using familiar material from the wisdom literature, simply inserting it as an exhortation in the midst of the analysis of his inverted society and the resulting frustration. If it is not a later insertion by a pious editor—and I believe it is not—then this unit must be read in light of Qoheleth's view of the world as we see it in the book as a whole.

By including this unit in the section on confronting the present with trust in God's grace, we can see the profound meaning of the text. As I pointed out at the beginning of this section, the text seeks to show the distance between the divine and the human: God is in heaven and we are on earth. To be more exact, it shows its readers the importance of understanding the limitations that are part of the human condition. It is important to Qoheleth to combat the feelings of impotence and frustration produced by human limitations. People fall into total frustration when they know that they cannot change things. Qoheleth is telling them that they are not God and therefore they should not feel helpless in their society. Rather they should adopt an attitude of respect for the divine, because it is a mystery beyond human understanding.

In the text Qoheleth asks his readers to be receptive to the mystery of God, not to hurry or be anxious, begging God for favors; for this attitude is also dehumanizing and demeaning. Rather, he wants them to let God reveal Godself in a way and at a time of God's choosing, and to trust God's grace in the midst of their absurd world.

The unit is made up of four admonitions: 5:1; 5:2-3; 5:4-5; and 5:6-7.

5:1 [Heb. 4:17]. The first admonition: Be careful and receptive when you approach God. The house of God refers to the temple; the phrase "guard your steps" is figurative, meaning to be careful (cf. Proverbs 1:15; 3:26; 4:27). Qoheleth asks people to be receptive, to listen to what God has to say. Better than sacrifice are the honesty and solidarity of the person offering it.

Qoheleth describes those who make sacrifices mechanically, without reflecting on their meaning, as fools. The prophetic and wisdom traditions also praise the attitude of the heart over the act of sacrifice (cf. Amos 5:21-25; Hosea 6:6; Isaiah 1; Micah 6:6-9; Jeremiah 7; Psalm 50; Sirach 34:18).[53] The last part of the verse is unclear; it may mean "they do not know how to do evil," or "they do not know that they are doing evil." Here evil may refer to the creation of a calamity.[54] According to Vílchez, Qoheleth is saying not that the fools are evil but that they are unaware.[55] And they certainly do not know how to do the right thing.[56]

5:2-3 [Heb. 5:1-2]. The second admonition: Let your words to God be brief and well chosen.[57] This idea is typical of the wisdom style in Israel and in other nearby cultures. The two verses continue the line of listening more than speaking and recognizing one's human limitations. In recognizing that God is God, we recognize that humans are human. Verses 2-3 insistently repeat the advice to be of few words, well thought-out ("let not your heart be quick to utter . . ."). Those who say a lot in their prayers are thinking neither of God nor of the meaning of their words; they do not even have time to think about themselves. They are charlatans, concealing their real identity and the reality around them. In contrast, silence and a few well-chosen words reveal their identity and reality, and also reveal honest reflection. Matthew 6:7 presents the same idea.

Verse 3 is a proverb, of which only the second part is relevant to the context; it speaks of the uselessness of many words.[58] But the first part of the proverb may be in line with Qoheleth's thinking elsewhere in the book, where he speaks of excessive work that disturbs sleep (2:23).[59] Or he may mean that excessive zeal in petitionary prayer causes dreams or illusions that the prayer will be accepted.[60] The meaning is unclear to readers in the present. This is a type of proverb in which the second truth is supported by an analogy (there are similar sayings in Proverbs 11:16; 25:23, 27, 17): just as dreams come from many cares, so also the voice of a fool comes from many words.[61]

5:4-5 [Heb. 5:3-4]. The third admonition: Keep your vows. Qoheleth takes this almost literally from Deuteronomy 23:22-23. An ignorant person makes vows lightly and does not fulfill them. Unlike Deuteronomy, Qoheleth is not encouraging his readers to make vows to God. On the contrary, he considers it better not to promise anything to God than to be irresponsible about commitments. Such irresponsibility shows a lack of seriousness about God, about oneself, and about the reason for which one makes a vow. Qoheleth is admonishing his readers to make their deeds consistent with their words. Consistency gives a person authority. God is pleased with such people.

5:6-7 [Heb. 5:5-6]. The fourth admonition: Do not sin with your mouth. Literally, 5:6 [Heb. 5:5] says, "Do not let your mouth cause your flesh to sin, or make your flesh blameworthy." "Flesh" refers to the whole person. The translation would then be, "Do not let your mouth make you sinful." Again Qoheleth is warning about the consequences of speaking negligently. He may be referring to false testimony, swearing thoughtlessly, or blaspheming. It was common to profess ignorance in order to be absolved of lying; for Qoheleth it is the same as lying. One must be in control and accept responsibility for any error committed in the act of speaking. To say that one acted wrongly out of ignorance is not to take one's own actions seriously. Qoheleth is challenging the maturity of people's relationship with God, which requires consistency and dignity. Here "messenger" or angel probably refers to the priest or official in charge of the temple. It may also refer to God, as in other passages of the Bible. Qoheleth's intolerance toward this kind of person is portrayed as the intolerance of God, who is angry toward God's creatures and destroys their works. "The work of your hands" may refer to the fruit of labor.

Verse 7 [Heb. v. 6] is unclear; the three nouns appear without a verb. What is clear is the end: "fear God." This phrase, already used in 3:14, synthesizes the meaning of the whole unit. The behavior Qoheleth proposes in a situation of total frustration and helplessness is to recognize that human beings are not

God; they have limitations. By recognizing this, they can participate in history more wisely and effectively. The unit invites readers in Qoheleth's time to keep a wise silence before God, to be consistent, and to let the mystery of God be revealed. Before God they should not be in haste, either with their mouth or in their hearts; rather they should be receptive to God's mystery. Many words, dreams (nightmares), and absurd situations alienate and numb the human consciousness. In contrast, the fear of God helps people to distinguish between God and God's creatures; this is a first step toward reordering the inverted reality.

THE GRIEVOUSNESS OF RICHES
(5:8-20 [Heb. 5:7-19])

In this unit and the next one, Qoheleth again looks critically at what happens under the sun in his society. Injustice against the poor happens not by God's will or by nature but by a sociopolitical system that runs on corruption.

It is true that the oppressed suffer greatly because of their economic needs; but in this unit Qoheleth focuses on the grievous ill that money causes to those who waste their life in a struggle for goods. The accumulation of wealth produces unhappiness for everyone, but in 5:10-20 [Heb. 5:9-19] he is addressing those whose riches bring them misfortune. He offers several reasons: their perennial dissatisfaction, sleeplessness, vulnerability in business, uselessness, suffering. I have divided the unit into four fragments: 5:8-9 [Heb. 5:7-8]; 5:10-12 [Heb. 5:9-11]; 5:13-17 [Heb. 5:12-16]; and 5:18-20 [Heb. 5:17-19].

Institutionalized Greed (5:8-9 [Heb. 5:7-8])

8If you see in a province the oppression of the poor and the violation of justice and right, do not be amazed at the matter; for the high official is watched by a higher, and there are

yet higher ones over them. ⁹But all things considered, this is
*an advantage for a land: a king for a plowed field.**

In 3:16 and 4:1 Qoheleth described the suffering of the
oppressed and the invertedness of society. In 5:8, he describes
the hierarchical bureaucratic system of his society. He is probably referring to the Ptolemaic system, since as M. Rostovtzeff
says, over time the Ptolemaic bureaucracy has degenerated into
an instrument of intolerable, dishonest oppression.[62] The gov-
erning officials cover up their bad works, one by one. They
never hear the protests of the poor against their abuse of authority; rather they protect each other, right up to the highest rank.
Under Qoheleth's sun there is no one to turn to in search of justice; they are all taking bribes, they are all practicing corruption.
So the author advises readers not to be amazed at the perversion
of justice in their time, for it is the consequence of a corrupt
administrative system. According to Kathleen A. Farmer, the
poor are oppressed and their rights are denied because at every
level of authority, the officials are not concerned with them but
are out to please the higher-ranked officials.[63]

"The province" probably refers to Syro-Phoenicia, since at
the time of the Ptolemaic empire Judea belonged to that
province, geographically defined for legal purposes.[64]
"Watched by" (Hebrew: *shomer*) connotes protection as well as
control.[65] According to James L. Crenshaw, it also has overtones of hostility.[66]

Some people believe that the one of highest rank who
watches the others is God. This interpretation is valid only if
one understands the text in a more optimistic context. Ogden
chooses it over more common readings, such as the one I have
described above. In a context of violent oppression and larceny,
people need to believe that an official of justice will do justice; if
that one does not, someone else will, and if not, God is watch-

---

* The Spanish version used by the author renders v. 9 as follows: "Moreover,
the benefit of the land is for all; the king himself is subject to the fields."

ing above them all. Although this interpretation would fit well in the section we are analyzing (on facing the future with trust in God's grace), I believe that a critique of the bureaucracy and complicity among officials is more consistent with Qoheleth's thinking.

Verse 9 is the hardest to interpret in the whole book, because the Hebrew is so unclear. Literally it says that the benefit of the land is in everything a king of the cultivated land (or of the land that serves the king). This has been interpreted in different ways. Ravasi suggests the following: ". . . a country is more just if the king is attentive to agrarian policy, to a correct distribution of the fields, to a struggle against latifundios and against the neglect of the land."[67] If the king does so, he is helping to reorganize a society turned upside down by the corruption of his subjects.

Another interpretation is an affirmation of justice, and a critique of the king's role: the benefit of the land is for all, despite the fact that the king takes control of the product (helps himself to it).[68] Yet another: everyone—the officials and the king—takes advantage of the peasants' land. This interpretation connects well with the preceding verse.

The Pitfalls of Money (5:10-12 [Heb. 5:9-11])

> [10]*The lover of money will not be satisfied with money; nor the lover of wealth, with gain. This also is vanity.*
> [11]*When goods increase, those who eat them increase; and what gain has their owner but to see them with his eyes?*
> [12]*Sweet is the sleep of laborers, whether they eat little or much; but the surfeit of the rich will not let them sleep.*

Money is a trap when it becomes the purpose of life. The meaning of this fragment comes from the dissatisfaction one feels with the accumulation of capital. There are three reasons for this dissatisfaction. The lover of money never gets enough (v. 10); the goods do not benefit their owner, because others consume them (v. 11); the rich do not rest or sleep well at night (v. 12).

Qoheleth quotes a proverb (v. 10 [Heb. v. 9]) to describe the reality that those who have more want more. The love of money is the root of all kinds of evil, says the writer of 1 Timothy 6:10—that is, when money is placed above other values and one's life is directed toward that goal. This is what Qoheleth calls *hebel,* the absurd. There is no human fulfillment in an obsessive concern for money.[69] Just as enslaving, fruitless toil is alienating, so also the concern for money leads to the annihilation of all that is human. There is a popular Latin American saying: "the frog puffed itself up until it burst, trying to be a cow." Like Job, Qoheleth rejects the wisdom tradition that considers riches a blessing from God. For Qoheleth, riches cause suffering rather than pleasure.

Verse 11 [Heb. v. 10] depicts a scene common among the rich of that time (and ours). The rich achieve prestige and must then maintain it at great expense: they are surrounded by friends, parasites whom they must please by means of banquets, gifts, and favors. The richer they are, the more "guests" they have. The cost of maintaining their honorific position by wealth is so great that the only satisfaction they can achieve is to look at their goods without enjoying them. That is not a real gain. The rich are deceiving themselves. They lose the best years of their lives working for others, without the human fulfillment that comes from enjoying everyday simplicity. They sacrifice their humanity for something that does not bring happiness.

Qoheleth contrasts this with the life of the humble worker who knows how to enjoy life (v. 12 [Heb. v. 11]). By not making money the only concern and purpose for life, the worker can live as a free person and sleep at night. The rich, in contrast, suffer insomnia because of all the worries caused by an abundance of wealth.

The text should not be misinterpreted as an ideology that encourages workers to be satisfied with little to eat, by describing the downside of wealth. Qoheleth has already said that workers have the right to enjoy the fruits of their labor. This unit is denouncing the irrationality of the social sector that, fascinated with the Hellenistic economic model, has devoted itself to maximum efficient production. This leads him also to denounce the dehumanization of falling into the trap of accumulating wealth.

It is said that in a country of sharp contrasts, no one can sleep. The poor—the majority—do not sleep because they are hungry, and the rich do not sleep because they know it. Qoheleth prefers the modest life of the workers, who perhaps eat well with their friends one day and eat little but enjoy it the next. This is an attitude toward life in which people are subjects, not the objects, of money. It is like the attitude of Ross and Gloria Kinsler, who seek to promote an awareness that "enough is enough."[70]

The Accumulation of Wealth Is an Unhealthy Calamity (5:13-17 [Heb. 5:12-16])

> [13]*There is a grievous ill that I have seen under the sun: riches were kept by their owners to their hurt,* [14]*and those riches were lost in a bad venture; though they are parents of children, they have nothing in their hands.* [15]*As they came from their mother's womb, so they shall go again, naked as they came; they shall take nothing for their toil, which they may carry away with their hands.* [16]*This also is a grievous ill: just as they came, so shall they go; and what gain do they have from toiling for the wind?* [17]*Besides, all their days they eat in darkness, in much vexation and sickness and resentment.*

The point of this fragment is the uselessness of wealth amid the vicissitudes of the economic world and the great disillusionment one feels at the end of a life of vain, enslaving toil. Great evil, anger, and resentment are the result of a life that is meaningless, because it is devoted to accumulation.

Verse 13 classifies the accumulation of riches as a grievous ill. One expects enjoyment to come from wealth, but it does not.

Accumulation is self-destructive, Qoheleth insists. Verse 14 may refer to financial dealings that were characteristic of the new economic order in which Qoheleth lived. Investments were unsafe. Perhaps he meant an investment in which speculation played a central role. In the context of a commercial boom, financial security was unpredictable.[71] For Qoheleth, a life subject to financial ups and downs is not a life. And when the investment is lost, it is not only the owner who loses but also his descendants, for whose benefit he was supposedly working. Thus Qoheleth emphasizes the uselessness of wasting one's life for riches, even when the riches are for one's heirs, since one can never be sure they will be able to inherit it.

Verse 15 speaks about people in a different situation, although like v. 14 it refers to a son. Indeed he is speaking of everyone who works for the purpose of accumulating the fruit of their labor: nothing is left in their hands, as he says twice (vv. 14 and 15). Although by linking the two verses the text may be referring both to the father who was working for money, and to the son, Qoheleth is trying to emphasize—using the words of Job 1:21—that riches are not important in life, since one is born poor and dies poor. Nakedness is a metaphor for material poverty.[72] The idea of being born naked and dying naked often appears in other cultures and popular sayings. A Latin American saying makes the same point: "I was born naked, I will die naked; I don't win and I don't lose."

The fact that one has wasted one's life filling one's hands, and ends up with empty hands, is described in v. 16 as an unhealthy calamity (*ra'ah holah*) (NRSV: "grievous ill").[73] What one is doing is toiling for the wind (*ruah*).[74] Verse 16 repeats with a note of resentment that one comes to life and leaves it, and nothing has changed for the accumulator. The rhetorical question at the end of the verse repeats Qoheleth's concern from earlier chapters (1:3; 2:22; 3:9). Ravasi puts it in these words: "What is the point of doing so much for this demanding idol, money, when the idol turns out to be so fragile and treacherous?"[75]

There is no advantage for human beings in enslaving toil.

The phrase "this also is a grievous ill" is placed in a position of equivalence with "this also is *hebel*" (5:10 [Heb. 5:9]).

Verse 17 is unclear in Hebrew and is rendered differently from one version to another. But the idea is clear. Three emotional states characterize the slave to money during the process of accumulation and after the fall into bankrupcy. During their life (all their days) "they eat in darkness, in much vexation and sickness and resentment."[76] To eat in darkness all their days may mean consuming their life in the midst of sadness. It may also be literally interpreted as eating food in an unhappy way, in an atmosphere very different from the one proposed in the following verses (18-20 [Heb. 17-19]).

It Is Good and Beautiful to Eat, Drink, and Enjoy the Fruit of Labor (5:18-20 [Heb. 5:17-19])

> [18]*This is what I have seen to be good: it is fitting to eat and drink and find enjoyment in all the toil with which one toils under the sun the few days of the life God gives us; for this is our lot.* [19]*Likewise all to whom God gives wealth and possessions and whom he enables to enjoy them, and to accept their lot and find enjoyment in their toil— this is the gift of God.* [20]*For they will scarcely brood over the days of their lives, because God keeps them occupied with the joy of their hearts.*

Here again is Qoheleth's proposal of choice, immediately following his discussion of the way in which people become things when they are enslaved to money. The misfortune of riches leads him to insist on what he thinks will lead to human fulfillment in his time: to enjoy intensely the everyday moments that make one happy, that give primacy to the human being as a subject. God gives the gift of life and also the ability to enjoy it. Human beings enslave themselves or allow themselves to be enslaved by a system based on profit. They lose the perspective of their vocation as humans, free to enjoy God's gifts. If they do not make use of the gifts of everyday joy and happiness and the life-giving value of material goods (to eat and drink and find enjoyment in the fruit of their toil), they fall into the trap of a dehumanizing logic. In this unit, that logic is the desire for money; it is the logic of having rather than the logic of being. Qoheleth's proposal in face of a dehumanizing situation is to live God's grace in the intimacy of everyday life.

Curiously, in v. 19 he lowers his tone toward the rich. Riches are a gift of God; that was also the view of the wisdom tradition. The difference is that Qoheleth is advising them not to make riches their goal in life but to enjoy life to whatever degree they can; to accept and enjoy the portion they receive from the fruit of their labor. This is hard to do, as he has warned in v. 10 [Heb. v. 9]. If they succeed, they can avoid the fate of the accumulator described in v. 17 [Heb. v. 16]; heartfelt happiness enables them to withstand the absurdity imposed by the dehumanizing logic of the world. The attitude recommended in v. 20 [Heb. v. 19] stands over against that of v. 17 [Heb. v. 16]: refusing to "brood over the days of their lives," because God keeps them occupied with joy, is a defense mechanism that enables them to resist the absurd.

THE UNHAPPINESS OF NOT BEING ABLE TO ENJOY LIFE (6:1-12)

For Qoheleth, one of the greatest obstacles to human fulfillment is the inability to enjoy life while one is living. The inverted society not only frustrates people's desires; it also dehumanizes them by inhibiting their ability to enjoy what they have. The same is true of those who become slaves of money. Unbridled greed and competitiveness do not allow human beings to be truly human, because they do not take the time for daily enjoyment of the fruit of their labor. Thus, injustice and greed cause both victims and victimizers to lose their human consciousness and to become objects or slaves.

In this unit (6:1-12) Qoheleth focuses on that "evil" (ra^c). He sees it as common, and for him there is nothing worse than being unable to taste happiness, at least momentarily. Nothing else matters. I have divided this unit into three sequences (6:1-6; 6:7-9; 6:10-12); the title of each, taken from a popular saying, reflects its central concern. The last sequence is not directly related to chapter 6, but it serves as a conclusion for the whole second section (3:1-6:12). In order to be happy in a situation of total frustration, human beings should recognize their human condition. In this situation, the desire to be God almighty is dehumanizing because it leads to helplessness. Even the most elaborate arguments cannot definitively answer our question about the historical future.

The Only Way to Get Anything out of Life Is by Enjoying It (6:1-6)

> *6¹There is an evil that I have seen under the sun, and it lies heavy upon humankind: ²those to whom God gives wealth, possessions, and honor, so that they lack nothing of all that they desire, yet God does not enable them to enjoy these things, but a stranger enjoys them. This is vanity; it is a grievous ill. ³A man may beget a hundred children, and live many years; but however many are the days of his years, if he does not enjoy life's good things, or has no burial, I say that a stillborn child is better off than he. ⁴For it comes into vanity and goes into darkness, and in darkness its name is covered; ⁵moreover it has not seen the sun or known anything; yet it finds rest rather than he. ⁶Even though he should live a thousand years twice over, yet enjoy no good—do not all go to the same place?*

The inability of human beings to enjoy or to consume their own goods is described as pathetic in vv. 1-2. Qoheleth frames it as "an evil" at the beginning of v. 1, and as absurd and grievous —literally in the Hebrew, "a severe illness"[77]—at the end of v. 2. He classifies this illness as widespread and common (*rabah*)[78] among human beings. Although it can happen to anyone, here the evil is more evident because it refers to the rich who have achieved wealth, possessions, and honor,[79] and all that their throats desire,[80] but who are not able to enjoy it.[81] In earlier verses Qoheleth has mentioned several reasons: labor without rest, the greed of accumulation, or the fact that another has taken possession of the fruit of labor. Here he may be referring to the last of these; a foreigner or stranger is enjoying the goods. The Hebrew word *nokry* usually refers to a non-Jewish foreigner;[82] here I believe it should be assigned that meaning, although most commentators take it to mean a stranger, anyone outside the family circle. In the third century B.C.E., foreigners —especially Greeks—took advantage of the Judeans to enrich themselves.[83] This is precisely the source of Qoheleth's anger in 2:21.

Qoheleth shows us an arbitrary God, the cause of this inability to enjoy. God gives the gift of riches, but to some people he doesn't give the ability to enjoy them. In Qoheleth's time God was seen as the source of both good and bad things. He does not understand this absurd activity of God; that is why in 6:10 he acknowledges that it is impossible to dispute with or reason against God. In 3:11 he recognizes more calmly that God's works under the sun are an impenetrable mystery.

But Qoheleth is clearly questioning the wisdom tradition, which affirms God's goodness or rewards to the righteous, as exemplified in riches. Riches are seen as blessings. For Qoheleth they are not blessings; rather they cause illness and evil, when for any reason they are not enjoyed or used from day to day.

Now his critique becomes even more radical. Verse 3 brings in two traditional ways of describing the greatest blessing that God bestows: a large family and a long life. Here is a new comparison, which to most people would be startling and scandalous: a stillborn baby is better off than a human being with a large family and a long life. Job's miserable life led him to a similar conclusion (Job 3:16). Qoheleth's reasoning comes from not having enjoyed what is good in life and therefore not taking satisfaction in length of life. Thus Qoheleth pursues, now in a more radical vein, the point he has been making throughout the book: the affirmation of real, everyday life is the most important value for human beings, whose humanity is unfulfilled in situations of total frustration.

Qoheleth adds another reason why the stillborn is better off: it does not have a proper burial. Not enjoying life and not being buried go together.[84] The reason for this is not clear. Whybray believes it may be an object lesson close to the first readers of the text. Perhaps it refers to a person well known in his time, with the above-mentioned characteristics, who died and was not buried, as criminals were not.[85] That would have had an impact on the readers. In any case, he is describing an unexpected humiliation at the end of life.[86]

Thus it is clear that, for Qoheleth, quality of life is more important than length of life without enjoyment.

Verses 4-5 invoke the metaphor of the stillborn baby. It represents nothingness, emptiness or meaninglessness, although it does have the movement of coming and going. It comes to existence without seeing the sun, or knowing (the events of history), since it has no consciousness of itself. Nor are others conscious of its existence, so it has no name or identity.[87] The darkness covers its name—that is, no one keeps its memory. It is accursed, as in Psalm 58:8 [Heb. v. 9]).

Verse 6 goes from metaphor to hyperbole, doubling the thousand-year life span. Not even two thousand years of life under the sun would be satisfying, if it was an empty and flavorless life. At the end of the verse Qoheleth brings in the event that comes inexorably to all: death. A human being comes to the same end as a fetus, a beast (3:19), or a fool (2:16). In view of this tragic end, Qoheleth hopes his readers will turn toward the search for a better quality of life here and now.

"Place" at the end of v. 6 is a euphemism for *sheol*, the place of the dead.

A Bird in the Hand Is Worth a Thousand on the Wing (6:7-9)

> [7]*All human toil is for the mouth, yet the appetite is not satisfied. *[8]*For what advantage have the wise over fools? And what do the poor have who know how to conduct themselves*

before the living? ⁹Better is the sight of the eyes than the wandering of desire; this also is vanity and a chasing after wind.

Verses 7-9 are a summary of Qoheleth's thought. In vv. 7 and 9a he quotes two familiar proverbs; in vv. 8a and 8b he repeats his rhetorical question about the advantage that some people have over others, and v. 9 closes with his negative, sorrowful evaluation of his reality.

There are four meanings here. Verse 7 refers back to the cyclical, enslaving logic introduced in 1:4-11. The saying describes the enslaving toil (*ᶜamal*) of human beings to satisfy their mouth[88]—that is, hunger. But hunger keeps coming back because the throat is never filled,[89] and one has to keep on working to fill it. The same thing happens to lovers of money: they are never satisfied (5:10 [Heb. 5:9]). Thus life is presented as meaningless; human beings cannot perceive themselves as subjects, as persons capable of consciousness and fulfillment. Here there is an implicit parallel with the monotonous movement of the cosmos, seen in 1:7: the rivers go to the sea, but the sea is never filled.

The second meaning appears in v. 8a and b. Indirectly Qoheleth is saying that it is not worth trying very hard to be wise or to conduct oneself well in life. This is because there is only a relative difference between the wise and the foolish. First, in an inverted society like Qoheleth's there is no real purpose in being wise, because the righteous are treated as if they were wicked, and the wicked as if they were righteous (cf. 7:15; 8:14). Second, the wise and the foolish have the same destiny: death, which makes no distinction among persons (cf. 2:14-17). The connection between the two sentences in v. 8 is not clear.[90] The clause "who know how to conduct themselves before the living" suggests an ability to face the events that occur under the sun, especially hostile ones. Apparently Qoheleth thinks of the poor as having this ability to face up to life.[91]

The first part of v. 9 quotes what may be a universal saying. In our popular culture it is "A bird in the hand is worth more than a hundred flying." This meaning is consistent with Qoheleth's proposal to enjoy everyday life and the benefits that are within one's reach. There is no point in devoting anguish and all one's energy to unattainable illusions. Life is better for those who try to enjoy what they have, here and now.

Qoheleth ends this reflection with his sentence on the absurdity of events under the sun: "This also is vanity and a chasing after wind." To enjoy what one has without expecting greater satisfaction is not the fundamental goal of humanization. It is simply what is feasible in situations of frustration. Thus, for a sage like Qoheleth, even though this is the best thing to do in a particular situation, it is still absurd and painful.

Choon-Leong Seow has discerned an interesting structure in 5:8 [Heb. 5:7] through 6:9.[92] It makes clear that the important thing is to enjoy life:

A. Those who are never satisfied (5:8-12 [Heb. 5:7-11])
B. Those who cannot enjoy (5:13-17 [Heb. 5:12-16])
C. What is good (5:18-19 {Heb. 5:17-18])
D. Enjoying the moment (5:20 [Heb. 5:19])
C'. What is evil (6:1-2)
B'. Those who cannot enjoy (6:3-6)
A'. Those who are never satisfied (6:7-9)

CONCLUSION (6:10-12)

The section ends with an emphasis on the limits of the human condition and the uselessness of arguing against God.

> [10]*Whatever has come to be has already been named, and it is known what human beings are, and that they are not able to dispute with those who are stronger.* [11]*The more words, the more vanity, so how is one the better?* [12]*For who knows what is good for mortals while they live the few days of their vain life, which they pass like a shadow? For who can tell them what will be after them under the sun?*

Verse 10 tries to make it clear that God is God and the human being is human, fragile and finite. God is more powerful than the creatures God has named. This is not new; Qoheleth says it has always been known. Human beings have nothing to gain by getting angry and taking God to court.[93] Trying to be God, and to change things as only God can, leads to total frustration. In contrast, by recognizing limitations as part of their own condition, human beings can acknowledge their frustration and move forward according to their own possibilities. To quarrel with the impossible only limits human action.

Instead of Job's scandalous litigation with God,[94] Qoheleth seeks another outcome for his time. Instead of arguing, he affirms life. Arguing leads nowhere, he says; it is inefficient and absurd, because there is so little chance of understanding reality and the events of life. God is a mystery that transcends human understanding. Empty rhetoric only reflects what human beings cannot attain: equality with God. Therefore, there is nothing better for human beings than to recognize the impossibility of comprehending the incomprehensible. The best part of wisdom is to acknowledge that we do not know. In another saying, "Those who know that they know not, are wise." Human wisdom means falling silent in the face of the inscrutable (5:3 [Heb. 5:4]); perhaps the only real dialogue is between God's silence and ours.

Qoheleth ends this fragment with two vital questions, which every sage was expected to answer for the people of Israel: What is good for mortals while they live their brief lives? And what events are coming under the sun? Qoheleth does not have the answer—no one has, or God has.

The narrator leaves the questions open; to get beyond this frustration, the reader can only say that there is a time and a season for everything. Meanwhile, the important thing is to affirm real, everyday life.

SECTION III

Discernment for Endurance and Choices in the Midst of Frustration (7:1-12:7)

Qoheleth's message so far has dealt with trusting God (Section II) in the face of total frustration (Section I), but he doesn't end his discourse there. He is a realistic sage. He understands the need to live "under the sun" day by day, hour by hour, minute by minute. Therefore he devotes much of this section to the importance of discernment and wisdom. He presents the best choices that can be made in everyday dilemmas. He offers practical advice or proverbs that gather wisdom for life from day-to-day experience, which he has constantly verified.

These are not dogmas. It would be impossible to dogmatize, for instance, our culture's common affirmation that "God helps those who get up early"—when it is equally true that "you can't make the dawn come by getting up early." When the horizons are closed, Qoheleth knows the importance of discerning when to get up early, and when not to be too anxious for the dawn. In situations of frustration it takes shrewdness to choose "the greater good and the lesser evil."

The important thing is life, and the joy of living. Although Qoheleth would like to be dead, or stillborn, in order not to see the violence that the oppressed suffer under the sun (4:2f.), he chooses life even when the horizons are closed (9:4-9). Believing that they will open again, since there is a time and season for everything, he proposes to live shrewdly so as not to hasten death. In a society where things go badly for the righteous and well for the wicked, wise and conscious persons know how to live with honesty and dignity, taking risks or sidestepping adversities to avoid a premature death (7:16f.). Since no one knows what will happen—the horizons block our view beyond the present—we must find our own way and follow it carefully (7:18; 11:4-6).

Besides offering a large body of advice, this section returns to themes he has raised before. Again he describes his inverted society, affirms day-to-day life and relationships, and remembers the inevitability of death. But he expands on them beautifully, with new elements in his invitation to live life (9:7-9), and in his final poem on the end of life (11:9-12:7). He can do this because when the horizons are closed, the only thing one knows of the future is that the thread will be cut between the living and the dead. But what matters to Qoheleth is not the moment of cutting itself; rather it is knowing that the moment exists. Because we know it is coming, we must affirm and enjoy life as early as possible, while there is still time.

Section III is made up of five units.

ACTING WITH DISCERNMENT (7:1-8:9)

This unit begins with the repeated phrase "it is better," or "it is worth more" (*tob min*), with overtones of sobriety and sadness (7:1-14). The unit ends with a clear affirmation of the frustration that comes from observing and analyzing events under the sun (vv. 8-9a). It is frustrating because the authority of one person over another causes the other's hurt (v. 9b). The unit is developed by means of concrete advice on how to act in situations of total frustration due to injustice, repression by the king, and the coming of death. Qoheleth's main contribution is to shed light on the day-to-day path through hardships and uncertainties: one should practice maturity, discernment, prudence, simplicity, and above all, wisdom. Those things enable one to avoid being crushed by unfavorable circumstances. Uncertainty requires discernment (7:14, 24; 8:7).

Enjoy the Good Days, Reflect on the Days of Adversity (7:1-14)

The first eight verses establish the sad rhythm of a hard life. Death, mourning, and sorrow are better than laughter and mirth in situations of frustration. Feasting, laughter, and the day of birth celebrate and legitimize an absurd system, if one is not conscious of the absurdity. In the pattern of "better than," Qoheleth's choices represent a coherent and honest answer to the prevailing perversion and oppression (7:29; 8:9). Verses 9-14 invite the reader to take things with maturity, not to let frustration make them bitter, and to make the best of it. "Keep your chin up." Thus he recommends enjoying the good days, and when the hard times come, reflecting and recognizing one's human limitations.

Moderation and Soberness Are Better Than Precipitousness and Extravagance (7:1-8)

> *7¹ A good name is better than precious ointment,*
>   *and the day of death, than the day of birth.*
> *² It is better to go to the house of mourning*
>   *than to go to the house of feasting;*
> *for this is the end of everyone,*
>   *and the living will lay it to heart.*
> *³ Sorrow is better than laughter,*
>   *for by sadness of countenance the heart is made*
>   *glad.*
> *⁴ The heart of the wise is in the house of mourning;*
>   *but the heart of fools is in the house of mirth.*
> *⁵ It is better to hear the rebuke of the wise*
>   *than to hear the song of fools.*
> *⁶ For like the crackling of thorns under a pot,*

so is the laughter of fools;
this also is vanity.
⁷*Surely oppression makes the wise foolish,*
and a bribe corrupts the heart.
⁸ *Better is the end of a thing than its beginning;*
the patient in spirit are better than the proud in
spirit.

This fragment seems to contradict Qoheleth's more favored refrain, which holds up eating and drinking as the best things one can do under the sun. Here, in vv. 7:1-4, he prefers the day of death to the day of birth, funerals to banquets, and mourning to feasting and laughter. We can only understand these proposals by reading them from two different viewpoints. The favored refrain urges us to live the present moments with intensity from day to day, in the midst of frustration, in order to affirm humanizing personhood in the face of the institutional system that causes the frustration. The sadness of vv. 7:1-4 and v. 6 is justified if we are living in alienation and celebrating an unjust system. Death, mourning, and sorrow are better than laughter, feasting, and the day of birth, if the latter march to the beat of an absurd system. Obviously Qoheleth was not fond of the great banquets that were attended or held by aristocracy of his time.

Precious ointment (v. 1) is an allusion to ostentatious and costly things. Birth refers to the beginning of life, when one is not yet aware of events under the sun and has not yet set out on the path of absurdity. The house of feasting (v. 2b) and the house of mirth (v. 4b) refer to collective celebrations, especially those of the rich, who do not know, or want to know, the truth of what happens under the sun. The participants in the banquet are fools (v. 4b). The song of fools is vacuous, like the crackling of thorns in the fire (v. 6); we can hear it as we read.¹ It is empty, meaningless laughter; he emphasizes that point by calling it vain (*hebel*).

Verses 2cd and 3b show why mourning and sorrow are better than feasting and laughter. Mourning reminds human beings of their limitations and inevitable death (v. 2c); those who go to funerals cannot forget their human condition and what is happening under the sun. The sadness caused by the events of history leads people to reflect on the truth (v. 3b); that reflection turns them into conscious human beings.

To enjoy bread and wine in the midst of frustration is a conscious response to a different truth, which stands over against the present, dehumanizing lie (2:24). This enjoyment contributes, as sorrow and death do, to the humanization of human beings; it allows them to feel like living subjects and not like objects of a system ruled by inverted laws. By looking death in the face, subjects are led to feel alive and to make use of their own life, which passes quickly.[2] Eating and drinking with enjoyment also lead persons to feel alive and to live the best they can. In this sense, ". . . is better than . . ." is a way of distinguishing the authentic from the inauthentic. The first line sets this tone: being (a good name) is better than appearance (precious ointment).[3]

To seek the truth of events under the sun means to shun adulation; one must prefer the rebuke of the wise (7:5).

Verse 7 speaks directly of oppression, one of the greatest causes of total frustration. In that situation of violent oppression against the poor, the wise do not let themselves be bribed (v. 7b), unless oppression has made them foolish (v. 7a). To know the truth of events causes sorrow (1:18).

The last two clauses in this fragment are not connected to each other. Verse 8 chooses the end of a thing over its beginning, because the beginning is marked by uncertainty, and in situations of frustration, uncertainty is annihilating. Nevertheless it is better to be honest with reality, even a painful reality, than to be like the proud who are above it all (v. 8b), unaffected by the absurd situation that exists under the sun.

The Greater Good, the Lesser Evil (7:9-14)

> [9] Do not be quick to anger,
> for anger lodges in the bosom of fools.

¹⁰ *Do not say, "Why were the former days better than*
  these?"
  For it is not from wisdom that you ask this.
¹¹ *Wisdom is as good as an inheritance,*
  an advantage to those who see the sun.
¹² *For the protection of wisdom is like the protection of*
  money,
  and the advantage of knowledge is that wisdom
  gives life to the one who posesses it.
¹³ *Consider the work of God;*
  who can make straight what he has made crooked?
¹⁴*In the day of prosperity be joyful, and in the day of*
adversity consider; God has made the one as well as the other,
so that mortals may not find out anything that will come
after them.

Verses 7:9-14 are all interconnected. Qoheleth is advising his readers to try to live happily in the midst of total frustration. It is useless to get excited without thinking. Unreflecting anger is a response of fools, not of the wise (7:9). In the same way, it is useless to spend one's life yearning for better days in the past; that is not the attitude of the wise (7:10). Living on good memories from the past does not help one to face the present. One must take on the present and find in what one has, something to dignify or improve the quality of life. Wisdom is better than riches; one must go on affirming this truth, because it is wisdom and not riches that gives life to those who possess it (7:12b). This does not mean that goods are to be deprecated; on the contrary, both wisdom and property are both advantageous (7:11). But if one must choose, wisdom is better than any material goods.

One should not be anxious or defeated in situations of total frustration. When we come to the conclusion that an inverted society cannot be transformed, we have to recognize the limits of what we can do; that is the point of v. 13. There is a popular saying that you can't get pears from an elm tree. Those who spend their life trying to harvest pears will be unhappy and will wander down the wrong road. The wise do not wish for what they know is impossible; rather they recognize that there is a time and a season for everything, as Qoheleth says elsewhere. You can't make the dawn come by getting up early.

There are good days and bad days. One must take advantage of the good ones. When a good day comes, we should enjoy it without hesitation or feelings of guilt; when a bad day comes, we should reflect on its meaning and its implications for everyone's happiness (7:14). Human fulfillment means recognizing that sometimes nothing can be done. Qoheleth often attributes these impossible situations to God; thus he says that the crookedness is God's work (v. 13); God made both the good days and the bad (v. 14). These are ways of expressing human helplessness in a context of total frustration, when transformation is impossible. Qoheleth knows well that the crookedness was caused not by God but by human beings (7:29). But since human beings cannot understand God's way of working, which permits situations of frustration, then in the last analysis God is responsible for everything; human wisdom cannot comprehend the reason for such dehumanizing events. In these situations Qoheleth proposes choosing what will enable one to endure and not be defeated. Everything gets harder when we cannot see the future.

"Everything in Moderation" (7:15-22)

15 In my vain life I have seen everything; there are righteous people who perish in their righteousness, and there are wicked people who prolong their life in their evil-doing. 16 Do not be too righteous, and do not act too wise; why should you destroy yourself? 17 Do not be too wicked, and do not be a fool; why should you die before your time? 18 It is good that you should take hold of the one, without letting go of the other; for the one who fears God shall succeed with both.

19 Wisdom gives strength to the wise more than ten rulers that are in a city.

*²⁰ Surely there is no one on earth so righteous as to do good
without ever sinning.*
*²¹Do not give heed to everything that people say, or you
may hear your servant cursing you; ²²your heart knows that
many times you have yourself cursed others.*

Verses 15-22 focus on the inverted society, where the righteous die like the wicked and the wicked live like the righteous.
In such a situation one has to be prudent; everything in moderation. Those who are too righteous will be treated like the
wicked; those who are very wicked will be seen, dishonestly, as
righteous. We must look for just the right level of goodness in
life, as another saying has it: "Not too high to get over, not too
low to get under." We don't give up seeking wisdom and discernment. Wisdom gives life (v. 12b) and strength (v. 19). But
we don't worry about being perfect, or about what others think
of us.

Qoheleth 7:15 contradicts the traditional theology. There is
no room, in the analysis that Qoheleth is able to make of his
society during his short life,[4] for the belief that the righteous are
given long life while the wicked perish for their actions. To be
honest with reality means recognizing that the righteous are
often worse off than the wicked. We have seen Job vehemently
complaining to God about this injustice. Qoheleth is not arguing with God, but simply looking for ways to survive in this context of total frustration.

Since the truth proclaimed by traditional wisdom does not
work out in practice, Qoheleth proposes an unexpected and
unorthodox solution: not to be too righteous or too wise, as the
sages advise, nor as wicked as fools are. He recommends moderation as a means of survival. Either extreme, at that time in his
society, leads to self-destruction (7:16-17). Our popular saying,
"It's not good to be too good," reflects that paradox.

In v. 18, "take hold of the one without letting go of the
other" means to "hedge one's bets," prudently keeping options
open even when one does not fully agree with them. The goal is

to survive in the present. The second phrase (7:18b) is an attempt to build the reader's confidence. To fear God, as we have said, means recognizing one's human limitations and thereby increasing self-confidence. In a "save-your-own-skin" society, those who act with discernment and moderation, trusting the mysterious God, will survive. What we need in that situation is not military or political power but realistic wisdom. Qoheleth believes that wisdom is stronger than the power of many rulers in a city (7:19). In that time, the city was a hostile environment for impoverished peasants, and for those who did not accept the Hellenistic culture.[5]

Verse 20 affirms a truth that everyone can agree with: no one in any society is perfectly righteous or sinless (7:20). Qoheleth brings in that truth to help readers accept his counsel of moderation, prudence, and shrewdness without feelings of guilt and discouragement. In a struggle for survival they should not give in to anguish or try anxiously to be perfect, always doing good and never seeing immediate results. An infinite struggle to be good can also be dehumanizing. Qoheleth is saying that "to err is human."

Verse 21, which may follow from v. 20, refers to the common problem of speaking ill of others. Here Qoheleth describes people who find out that a subordinate[6] has been talking about them behind their back. They should not get angry and punish the subordinate; no one should waste time worrying about gossip. Rather, they should remember that they have often done the same thing. Qoheleth is also insisting on the need to evaluate one's own behavior honestly.[7] Those who have command over others know in their conscience that they have often acted badly themselves (7:22).

The Absence of Wisdom and True Love (7:23-29)

23All this I have tested by wisdom; I said, "I will be wise," but it was far from me. 24That which is, is far off, and deep, very deep; who can find it out? 25I turned my mind to know and to search out and to seek wisdom and the sum of things, and to know that wickedness is folly and that foolishness is madness. [26]I found more bitter than death the woman who is a trap, whose heart is snares and nets, whose hands are fetters; one who pleases God escapes her, but the sinner is taken by her. [27]See, this is what I found, says the Teacher, adding one thing to another to find the sum, [28]which my mind has sought repeatedly, but I have not found. One man among a thousand I found, but a woman among all these I have not found. [29]See, this alone I found, that God made human beings straightforward, but they have devised many schemes.

This is one of the saddest fragments for Qoheleth's sorrowful soul. It reveals a deep, subjective wound caused by his failure to find perfect wisdom, with which to face a world of total frustration and to find the ideal woman, a genuine companion, with whom to be happy and live through the absurdity. Just as wisdom eludes him, the woman he longs for turns away. Without divine wisdom and without the beloved, he is lost. The key word is "find" (*matsa'*); it appears eight times in this brief fragment. Instead of what he wants to find, he finds the perversions (NRSV: schemes) caused by human beings (7:29).

"All this" in v. 23 refers to what he has studied so far by means of wisdom. He has done it honestly, trying to be wise. But he wisely recognizes his limitations. So much caution, to avoid being defeated, does not lead to human happiness. Qoheleth does not understand why creation is inverted. In v. 29 he concludes that it is caused by human beings, but he does not understand the enigma of history; why the creation God loves (Genesis 1; 2) has been turned around. Verse 24 speaks of the inaccessibility of wisdom, a common theme in wisdom literature (cf. Job 28). We see Qoheleth's despair of ever reaching it either horizontally (it is so far off) or vertically (it is so deep).[8] It is impenetrable; sometimes it raises its head, like a person whose otherness is a mystery.

In v. 25 he tries again to understand the inverted society through certainty of knowledge. Here, as in 1:17, he is very thorough. He wants the reader to know that he is giving not just simple opinions but conclusions based on a rigorous study of reality. The verse describes this process categorically: he proposes conscientiously (*leb*) to know (*yada͗*), investigate (*tur*), seek (*biqesh*) wisdom (*hokmah*) and reason (*heshbon*),[9] in order to understand (*yada͗*) the wickedness of folly. According to R. N. Whybray, Qoheleth is trying to go beyond practical common sense to find the meaning of total reality.[10]

Instead he finds the absence of authentic wisdom (v. 23) and of an authentic woman (v. 28). Absurd reality denies him the two things he wants most: a path and a purpose for life, and a person—in this case a woman—with whom to follow the path, a woman he can love freely and fearlessly, as at the beginning of creation (Genesis 2:22-25).

Verse 26 distills the bitterness of this frustrating reality. Qoheleth picks up ideas from the wisdom tradition about a certain type of woman (Proverbs 2:16-19; 5:4; 6:26). Even more bitter[11] and harder to accept than death is the type of woman who asphyxiates a man, who snares and chains him. Since those who follow God's paths cannot be alienated, such a woman is not able to eliminate their consciousness—to dehumanize them by the same logic as the society that cannot allow human interference. This type of woman is the feminine personification of folly, as opposed to the feminine personification of wisdom, which was also common in the wisdom literature. Here Qoheleth applies it to women, but it is also applicable to any group that tries to alienate the consciousness of others, disrespecting their otherness.

Qoheleth is saying that human relationships in his society have lost their original freshness and freedom. Intimate relationships of this sort turn life into bitter death, making the frustration unbearable.

In v. 27, Qoheleth[12] returns to his emphasis on a scientific search. He observes and examines every detail, one by one, in order to understand the whole. Finally he discovers what it is that he has been seeking and still wishes for: a woman, the special woman who stands out among thousands (v. 28). The text expresses melancholy and nostalgia rather than misogyny.

Thus Qoheleth comes up with two limited findings (vv. 28-29): only one (authentic?) man (*'adam*) in a thousand[13] and most of humanity (*'adam*) alienated, perverted,[14] far from the original, righteous, and simple (*yashar*) vocation that God gave them. Indeed, this is the only clear truth he can find to explain the frustrating world of his inverted society. In 3:11 he writes that God made everything suitable, but human beings could not understand God's work from the beginning to the end. Now he understands that God made human beings righteous, simple, and uncomplicated; it is they who turned society upside down and made human relationships complicated. This is why he cannot find the true person to love, with whom to share the intimacy of everyday life.

Wise Prudence in Tyrannical Times (8:1-9)

8[1] Who is like the wise man?
And who knows the interpretation of a thing?
Wisdom makes one's face shine,
and the hardness of one's countenance is changed.
[2] Keep the king's command because of your sacred oath.
[3] Do not be terrified; go from his presence, do not delay when the matter is unpleasant, for he does whatever he pleases. [4] For the word of the king is powerful, and who can say to him, "What are you doing?" [5] Whoever obeys a command will meet no harm, and the wise mind will know the time and way. [6] For every matter has its time and way, although the troubles of mortals lie heavy upon them. [7] Indeed, they do not know what is to be, for who can tell them how it will be? [8] No one has power over the wind to restrain the wind, or power over the day of death; there is no discharge from the battle, nor does wickedness deliver those who practice it. [9] All this I observed, applying my mind to all that is done under the sun, while one person exercises authority over another to the other's hurt.

This fragment advises Qoheleth's readers to conduct themselves wisely at a time when one human being dominates another in order to hurt the other (8:9). He speaks of three powers: that of the king (vv. 2-5), that of God (vv. 2, 6), and that of death (v. 8), all of which leave human beings helpless. Of these three, the hardest to bear is the power of the king, since it is the only one that can be escaped by human action. This exhortation is especially intended to help the king's subjects survive in times of tyranny, when the king does whatever he pleases (8:3c). For times like this we have a popular saying: "When the captain is in charge, the sailors don't give orders." In the face of God's power one can only leave the action to God, knowing that there is a time and a way for everything (8:6); God sets the conditions. In the face of the king's power, one must learn to behave wisely so as not to die prematurely. In the face of death, one must simply accept it realistically, since no one escapes death (vv. 7-8). Death will come in its time, but there is no reason to bring on premature death; in times of acute, tyrannical repression, one must learn to survive.

Verse 1 invites readers to seek wisdom. The spirit of survival is implicit in the form of expression. To know the interpretation of a thing is to know how to live, as v. 6 confirms. A face shining with wisdom reflects internal serenity, an absence of anguish, a sense of assurance in one's actions.

Those who do not know how to interpret the signs of the times wear a face of turmoil and anxiety.

Verses 2-5 refer to behavior toward the king. He is a tyrant; he does whatever he pleases (8:3c). His word is law, and no one can oppose it (v. 4). Irene Stephanus says that Qoheleth "must necessarily be an antimonarchist, because the one thing that best symbolizes the Ptolemaic empire is the king who not only is omnipotent, but also attributes divinity to himself according to the Egyptian tradition. The king is the definitive symbol of oppression."[15]

Under these conditions, Qoheleth recommends keeping the king's commands (v. 2) in order to "meet no harm" (v. 5). The heart of the wise—that is, the intellect—knows how and when to obey or resist the tyrant's commands (v. 5b).

"Your sacred oath" (v. 2) may refer to the custom of swearing loyalty to the king in the name of God, or in God's presence, as a sacred act.[16] According to Aarre Lauha, this was not a religious commitment. Qoheleth's advice is useful and realistic; it is not wise to go against the one who has power, because he also has legal authority.[17]

Verse 3 warns against leaving the king's presence in haste.* Perhaps it refers to counselors of the court who are afraid of the king, or who turn away in a sign of protest;[18] or to a deserter,[19] whose insecure or defiant behavior may cause suspicions of conspiracy. Tyrants know that their tyranny provokes opposition. For the same reason Qoheleth advises his readers not to conspire against the king, as v. 3b makes clear: "nor persist in a bad thing. . . ." Rather one must remember and believe that there is a time and a judgment** for everything,[20] since the situation is terribly troubling for mortals (v. 6). Despite his discourse against the monarchy, he is advising people not to risk their lives in times of *hebel,* when the horizons are closing in.

What troubles Qoheleth is that he cannot penetrate future events; he does not know what is coming and when it will come. He knows there will be another, a different time (3:1-8), but he does not know what and when—even though he is a sage. This is an implied criticism of the wisdom tradition with its assumed knowledge of everything: "for who can tell [mortals] how it will be?" (v. 7). Here Qoheleth is showing not only the advantages of being a sage, but also the limits of wisdom as a way of knowing and understanding the events that are to come.[21]

Verse 8 repeats what he has said about the limitations of humans as humans. The whole unit has emphasized the importance of recognizing limitations in order to make them bear-

---

* The Spanish version used by the author renders v. 3 as follows: "Do not hurry to go from his presence, nor persist in a bad thing; for he will do whatever he pleases. . . ."

** The author's version renders vv. 5b and 6a as follows: "the heart of the wise discerns the time and the judgment. Because for whatever you wish there is a time and a judgment. . . ."

able. Human beings are not the lords of the universe; they cannot control the breath of life or the wind.[22] They cannot prevent the arrival of death. No one can do that, not even the king. Thus the reader is reminded that the king is human too, and even if he considers himself all-powerful, he cannot prevail over death. His wickedness will not save him.[23]

Verse 9 is a conclusion for the fragment and the whole unit (7:1-8:9). This advice and the wisdom required are for a very specific time: a time of oppression, exploitation, and repression of some people by others. The time of the Ptolemies.

THE INVERTED SOCIETY (8:10-9:3)

This unit returns to earlier themes, with penetrating clarity and extraordinary forcefulness. Qoheleth again unmasks the distorted values of his society and questions the traditional theological theme of retribution. He rejects that doctrine as historically unverifiable, challenges it in debate, and then adopts it again, but with greater realism. In such a savage society he has no alternative but to hope that it will someday become real. These texts distill the bitter flavor of his frustration over the injustice of reality and over his inability to understand God's mysterious ways in rational terms. The unit begins with the pompous funerals of the wicked and ends with death as the destiny of all, without distinction between the righteous and the wicked. The logic of the unit, fraught with disappointment, is as follows:

1. The society is inverted in the extreme, and the delay in punishing the wicked increases its criminality (8:10-12a).
2. Nevertheless, Qoheleth still believes that God will do justice (8:12b and 13).
3. Even though at this historical moment the system of justice is upside down (8:14), to make the moment bearable and survive it well, in the midst of enslaving toil one must affirm real life with enjoyment, eating, and drinking (8:15).

4. For there is no rest from the task of conscientiously finding out what is happening under the sun; one must recognize that the human mind cannot understand the works that God does under the sun, or why God permits this invertedness (8:16-17).
5. Everything is absurd, especially because everyone comes to a common fate: death, without punishment or rewards (9:1-3).

The Inverted Society (8:10-15)

> [10]Then I saw the wicked buried; they used to go in and out of the holy place, and were praised in the city where they had done such things. This also is vanity. [11]Because sentence against an evil deed is not executed speedily, the human heart is fully set to do evil. [12]Though sinners do evil a hundred times and prolong their lives, yet I know that it will be well with those who fear God, because they stand in fear before him, [13]but it will not be well with the wicked, neither will they prolong their days like a shadow, because they do not stand in fear before God.
>
> [14]There is a vanity that takes place on earth, that there are righteous people who are treated according to the conduct of the wicked, and there are wicked people who are treated according to the conduct of the righteous. I said that this also is vanity. [15]So I commend enjoyment, for there is nothing better for people under the sun than to eat, and drink, and enjoy themselves, for this will go with them in their toil through the days of life that God gives them under the sun.

Verse 10 presents a number of exegetical problems. The Hebrew is illegible, and the translations vary accordingly.[24] Nevertheless the general meaning is clear, and it is repeated in v. 14: it is about the invertedness of the society, in which the wicked are treated as righteous and vice versa. This is my preferred reading. Qoheleth is an eyewitness to an everyday scene,[25] in which "the wicked"—those who practice injustice or corruption—are honored at their funerals.[26] Perhaps they are well-known politicians or magistrates. It seems as if the pompous ceremony and the rites could cancel all their crimes and perversions.[27] If the holy place means the temple,[28] then the religious authorities are probably involved.[29]

But worse than that, the inhabitants of the city forget the corrupt actions of the wicked. We might think, as Alphonse Maillot does, that there is nothing more frustrating for Qoheleth than the way the oppressed forget the injustice that has been done to them by their oppressors.[30] The Greek Septuagint (LXX) uses "praised" instead of "forgotten." This choice further dramatizes the situation; it means that the community praises, approves of, the dishonest acts committed by those who are now being buried. It is a painful absurdity, a terribly discouraging situation.

Some translations also add "the righteous" in the second part of the verse, to contrast with the wicked: the wicked are praised at their funerals, and the acts of the righteous are forgotten.[31] This is another absurd situation, like the one that follows.

Verse 11 introduces the element of delay in the execution of sentences against those who practice injustice. There are two consequences of delayed justice. First, it encourages people to continue acting unjustly, because there are no boundaries to hold them back. As long as they are not in any way harmed, they continue to benefit from their acts. In Qoheleth's view, impunity aggravates criminality. Second, when the victims see that justice is not done, they become frustrated and lose all hope of turning around the inverted society. Verse 11 does not say there is no sentence, only that it is too long delayed.

Qoheleth is probably thinking of the magistrates who do not execute justice speedily, and also of God, who delays establishing justice under the sun. It seems to be a veiled criticism of God.

Verses 12 and 13 are a vehement affirmation of faith in the face of the gross injustice practiced by sinners. "Though[32] sinners do evil a hundred times and prolong their lives,"[33] that does not invalidate the possibility of the inverted situation from returning to a just order when people accept the limitations set by God (vv. 12-13). Qoheleth is seizing this gloss—characteristic of the wisdom tradition, against which he has been struggling because of his everyday experience—with renewed energy. In a "save-your-own-skin" society, there is nothing left but to believe in something that goes beyond human possibilities. Faith in a just reordering, as Qoheleth sees it—that is, from the viewpoint of an absurd and frustrating reality—becomes an objective possibility. His critique of traditional beliefs is not against the affirmations themselves, which speak of justice, but rather against the superficiality (and therefore the unreality) with which they have been presented, without considering the complexity of human history.

Standing in fear before God means feeling one's human limits. Earlier in the book, "fear of God" meant recognizing our human limitations in order to participate more effectively in an uncertain world; now it means recognizing the boundaries between us and other humans, in order not to harm them. The fear of God is a sign of protection between one human and another. Thus Proverbs 16:6: "by the fear of the Lord one avoids evil."[34]

Long life for those who respect the rights of other human beings is the measure of an unperverted society.

In reality, Qoheleth's society is totally perverted; this is what he describes as *hebel*, absurd. It is so obvious that he repeats it in v. 14.[35] To believe that the righteous will have long life and the wicked will not doesn't change the fact that in practice it is the other way around. Verse 14 sharply refutes any doctrine of retribution that does not take into account the reality that everyday life is unjustly structured. If such a doctrine is affirmed without consideration for real life, it conceals the injustice. The divine justice to come is affirmed by faith, because one believes in a just God in spite of the inverted society.

Thus, the theory of retribution has merit, when it is considered as a promise or an ought-to-be. No one can accept a situation of impunity for the wicked and undeserved suffering for those who do good. Human beings need faith in an order where justice reigns. They need to affirm a reward for the just even when it is nowhere to be seen. This is a human necessity. The problem arises when such a doctrine becomes a dogma: that leads to a crisis of faith or wisdom and becomes a theory out of phase with reality. This is the critique of both Job and Qoheleth. Moreover, when faith in justice becomes a dogma, it is no longer a declaration of hope; rather it leads us to see the poor as sinners and the rich as blessed. When that happens, the doctrine is totally dissociated from the purpose of the proverbs and from the attitude of the ever-merciful Yahweh.

Verse 14 describes the real, the inverted reality; vv. 12-13 describe what should be and will be.

But when the inverted reality is experienced with such intensity, the resulting frustration over the slow justice of the magistrates and of God leads us to seek a reality different from *hebel*, a reality where we can experience something of the happiness of a noninverted society. That means enjoyment—eating and drinking. It is not enough to have faith in a future retribution, because we do not know when it will come, and our disappointment can be suffocating. We need to experience it in the now of real life. Therefore Qoheleth inserts in this unit (v. 15) the refrain that he has been repeating throughout the text, after each stage of investigating events under the sun. Faced with total frustration over the inverted society, he invites us to seek happiness earnestly in enjoyment, eating, drinking, and feasting throughout our God-given life. This everyday happiness should go along with enslaving toil. We do not have to wait for justice to be established before finding happiness; rather we must try to live life now, happily and humanely, fighting against the dehumanization of the inverted society in the hope of returning to a just order.

The Inability to Understand Events (8:16-17)

16When I applied my mind to know wisdom, and to see the business that is done on earth, how one's eyes see sleep neither

*day nor night, [17]then I saw all the work of God, that no one
can find out what is happening under the sun. However
much they may toil in seeking, they will not find it out; even
though those who are wise claim to know, they cannot find it
out.*

Verses 16-17 form the protasis (v. 16) and apodosis (v. 17) of
a conditional sentence.[36] The meaning is clear and characteristic
of Qoheleth; he has already affirmed the human impossibility of
understanding God's works in history.[37] A concerted effort has
led to this conclusion. In some ways this is a conclusion to the
preceding unit.[38]

That "one's eyes see sleep neither day nor night" can be
interpreted in two ways. It is often taken to refer to people's
inability to rest or to live with human dignity, because of "the
business that is done on earth": commerce or incessant labor
(cf. 2:23; 4:7-8). In reality they are not their own masters; they
are subjected to an anti-human rhythm. The other interpretation is suggested by Ogden. He understands Qoheleth as the
subject, whose eyes are drowsy by day and by night and cannot
see. This would be a metaphorical description of his inability
(day or night) to understand the events of history. He is like a
blind man.[39]

Verse 17 equates God's work with what is happening under
the sun. More explicitly, what he does not understand is the reason for events in the history of his inverted society: its evil,
oppression, and injustice,[40] and the designs of God, the source
of the universe and of everything that happens under the sun.
Qoheleth insists that they are incomprehensible and can never
be understood by human effort.

Three times, for emphasis, he expresses the uselessness of trying to discern the mystery of God's work: (1) "no one can find
out"; (2) "however much they may toil in seeking, they will not
find it out"; (3) "even though those who are wise claim to
know, they cannot find it out." Thus he ends with a challenge to
the sages of his time, who claimed perfect knowledge of all
things, even those on the horizon of the future.

The Injustice of a Common Destiny (9:1-3)

> *9¹All this I laid to heart, examining it all, how the righteous and the wise and their deeds are in the hand of God; whether it is love or hate one does not know. Everything that confronts them ²is vanity, since the same fate comes to all, to the righteous and the wicked, to the good and the evil, to the clean and the unclean, to those who sacrifice and those who do not sacrifice. As are the good, so are the sinners; those who swear are like those who shun an oath. ³This is an evil in all that happens under the sun, that the same fate comes to everyone. Moreover, the hearts of all are full of evil; madness is in their hearts while they live, and after that they go to the dead.*

The unit closes with a reference to themes mentioned at its beginning: dependency on God (for the righteous and wise), evil in the human heart, and the same death for all.

The texts are pregnant with painful and despairing uncertainty, because of events under the sun. There is some ambiguity, because the certainty that one grasps by faith[41] is joined with the uncertainty of events. After a conscientious analysis of reality ("All this I laid to heart, examining it all"), Qoheleth concludes that although he believes the righteous/wise[42] and their deeds are in the hand of God, he does not understand what God is doing. God may be acting out of love or hate, that is, acceptance or rejection[43]—in Gianfranco Ravasi's words, "out of solicitude or fiscal control"[44]—because the same mortal destiny awaits everyone.

"Everything is before them" is a hard phrase to understand.* In the interpretation I prefer, Qoheleth probably means that people are unable to discern, understand, or describe all that is and is happening in front of them. It is all beyond them. Qoheleth is challenging God's way: God is acting like an absent God.

---

* In the Spanish version used by the author, vv. 9:1c-2a are rendered as follows: "whether it is love or hate, human beings do not know; everything is before them. Everything happens in the same way to all. . . ."

Verse 2 shows the narrator's consternation and discouragement. Nothing one can do makes a difference in the destiny that awaits all types of people. He lists five antithetical pairs, covering the domains of justice and injustice, religion, and ethics. Such polar opposites are a conceptual tool characteristic of wisdom thought.[45]

We have seen that, for Qoheleth, the fact that there is no difference between the righteous and the wicked—even at the end of life—is a great calamity, a source of anguish for the wise and the righteous. Because they have the same mortal destiny, evildoers are encouraged in their malice and foolishness; they have no boundaries, for neither the courts nor God will soon punish those who practice injustice (cf. 8:11). Qoheleth is drawing a picture of the inverted society and, at the same time, indirectly questioning God's failure to intervene on the side of justice as the wisdom tradition expects. Qoheleth's basic protest is not against that tradition, when it says that God does justice to those who deserve it, but against the fact that the affirmation is not made real in the everyday life of his society, where the horizons have closed in.

AN ALTERNATIVE IN THE MIDST
OF TOTAL FRUSTRATION (9:4-12)

The overall purpose of this part is to remind us that despite the lack of distinction between good and evil deeds (9:1-3), it is better to live and to feel the vibrancy of life. Therefore we must live with a festive spirit, overcoming adversity, living by God's grace. This is a feasible way to resist the times of anti-human hostility,[46] and to combat the total frustration caused by the society. And we must do good, even without expecting a reward.

Here in the middle of the longer section we are studying (7:1-12:7), we find the refrain that Qoheleth has repeated in other central parts of his text. It is more complete this time. His fundamental point, as we have seen, is to affirm real and sensual life in the midst of frustration. Here it includes the company of the loved one. The refrain (9:7-9) is in the imperative mode: "Go, eat your bread with enjoyment. . . ." It is preceded by three verses (9:4-6) that point out the advantages of life over death and followed by three verses (9:10-12) that invite readers to accept life maturely and without complications, always doing the best they can, without getting mired down in the competition for first place in everything. The reason he advocates for accepting life with simplicity is the inevitability and unpredictability of the moment of death. The center of the unit presents a viable alternative: to make a feast of everyday life (vv. 7-9).

A Living Dog Is Better Than a Dead Lion (9:4-6)

> [4]*But whoever is joined with all the living has hope, for a living dog is better than a dead lion. [5]The living know that they will die, but the dead know nothing; they have no more reward, and even the memory of them is lost. [6]Their love and their hate and their envy have already perished; never again will they have any share in all that happens under the sun.*

Qoheleth ended the preceding fragment with the universality of death, in an inverted society where there is no distinction between the good and the bad (9:3). Here (9:4) for the first time Qoheleth clearly and explicitly chooses life over death, in spite of the bad times. He describes it as a certainty or security (*bitahon*),[47] a rare term that occurs only in 2 Kings 18:19 (repeated in Isaiah 36:4). Of course the certainty is there because one is alive, as in the popular saying, "Where there's life there's hope." Qoheleth uses (or perhaps he coined) the aphorism about the dog, meaning that no matter how miserable one's life is, it is better than even an honorable death. In the Near East a dog was looked down upon, and a lion was seen as the king of beasts (as it is today). Some see irony in vv. 4 and 5. But no; in our reading it is an affirmation—albeit a grudging one—of life in the midst of adversity. Verses 7-9 will confirm this reading.

In verses 5-6 Qoheleth describes five disadvantages of the dead. They know nothing; they have no more reward; their memory is lost;[48] their human passions of love, hate, and rivalry have died; and they will never again have their share (*heleq*) in human history. In 2:10, 3:22, 5:18, and 9:9, *heleq* was the share of enjoyment in eating and drinking, in the midst of enslaving toil.

Because of all these disadvantages related to the meaning of life itself, vibrant and pulsating through the body, we must seek life and enjoy it. And we must do it before death comes. The living know that someday they will die (v. 5a); therefore they must learn to live in the here and now.

Life Is for Living! (9:7-10)

> [7]*Go, eat your bread with enjoyment, and drink your wine with a merry heart; for God has long ago approved what you do.* [8]*Let your garments always be white; do not let oil be lacking on your head.* [9]*Enjoy life with the wife whom you love, all the days of your vain life that are given you under the sun, because that is your portion in life and in your toil at which you toil under the sun.* [10]*Whatever your hand finds to do, do with your might; for there is no work or thought or knowledge or wisdom in Sheol, to which you are going.*

It seems the only way out for Qoheleth is to reject the present by taking it on positively, affirming and living what the present cannot offer—rest, enjoyment, shared food—following a rhythm in which chronological time counts for nothing. This would be like living eternity in ordinary time, without taking time into account because we are not counting the minutes. Time is not money here, as it is in the marketplace, the bank, the stock exchange, and the workplace of enslaving toil. What counts here is the throat, and the shared joy of the feast. What counts are living bodies and earthly life, before the coming of eternal death.

Up to this point, the refrain has been presented as simple advice. Here, in 9:7-9, it is in the imperative mode. It has the tone of an urgent invitation, perhaps because death is lurking nearer; the theme of death is sounded in the verses preceding and following the refrain.

Eating bread and drinking wine are among the fundamental necessities of human life. There is delight in the process of eating and drinking. Therefore he insists that it be done with enjoyment, with true pleasure (*besimhah, beleb tob*). That is a way of opposing the dehumanizing rhythm of the Ptolemaic empire, which focused attention on the process of production. Human beings were seen as objects producing objects, and not as full subjects. Sharing a joyful meal (v. 9) is humanizing.

This humanizing act is pleasing to God.[49] God enjoys the enjoyment of God's creatures. Food and drink are gifts of God, and a right of human beings. Therefore humans should be joyful without feelings of remorse or guilt.

God is happy and approves of the work of God's creatures. The word "to approve" or "take pleasure" can refer to the past, present, and future. That God has already approved the works of humans (v. 7) does not mean that everything people do, have done, or will do is agreeable to God; rather, God accepts people by grace, and they can freely enjoy God's gifts. This is an exceedingly liberating message, in the context of the rigors of the temple during Qoheleth's time. Taking together the Ptolemaic society with its demand for production and the Jewish priestly society with its demand for constant purification (because it considers many human actions impure), the resulting frustration can lead to suicide. In this sense, by saying that God delights in human pleasure, Qoheleth may be making a veiled criticism of the priestly system of sacrifice in the Jerusalem temple.

Verse 8 insists on the festive attitude that human beings should adopt toward life. It was common in Egypt and Mesopotamia to dress in white and anoint the head with oil before going to a banquet. "Let your garments always be white" means to be festive for every possible occasion.

Thus, without making it explicit, by this affirmation of life Qoheleth is reminding us of the eschatological banquet, the utopian sign of new times in Isaiah 62:9.

Here woman appears for the second time, this time in a positive tone; he is referring to the beloved, not the suffocating woman. He invites readers to share life joyfully with the woman they love.[50] In a modern reading it might be put inclusively: "with the person you love," woman or man. "Live life" can be translated, "enjoy life." The word "see" is used in the Hebrew, with the connotation of experiencing. And the invitation is for "all the days," that is, your whole life, since it is so short. *Hebel* probably refers here to the ephemerality of human existence in history; Qoheleth will soon speak again of death. The Hebrew repeats "all the days of your vanity"; his emphasis is surely on taking every possible advantage of life because it is too short. In Graham Ogden's view, "that" (*'asher*) in the phrase "that [God has] given you" may refer not to days but to the woman. In this interpretation the woman is a gift of God, and he is therefore exhorting his readers to seek her love and to treat her as a gift of God.[51]

This whole, corporeal, pleasurable experience is seen as a gift of God and also as a right of all people. First, because it is a gift of God; also, because it rightfully belongs to human beings for all the work they do under the sun. It is their portion, their payment.

We must remember that this proposal for everyday life is not coming from an individualistic, isolated person who avoids all company but that of the woman he loves. Qoheleth argues strongly for unity with others; relationships of solidarity give strength and enable people to resist hostility (cf. 4:9-12). Here he is proposing a rhythm of life that favors people as human beings, against one that favors economic, political, or social institutions. He is describing a quality of life different from that proposed by the Ptolemies, or even by the Jewish society.

There are echoes of this proposal in other cultures. Many commentators have noted the similarity with *Gilgamesh* (2000 B.C.E.), which speaks of children, dancing, and games. "You

Gilgamesh, fill your belly, enjoy by day and by night. Celebrate a joyful feast every day. Day and night, you must dance and play! Let your garments be brightly colored, wash your hair, bathe in water. Attend to the little one who takes your hand. Let your wife take delight in your bosom!" (X,3)[52]

A Nahuatl poem of the sixteenth century, collected in Huexotzincgo, offers a similar alternative in the face of death. The poet says that the only viable solution is to live the present, overcoming anguish with songs, without ceasing to ask the reason for life. "For only a short time, like the magnolia flower, have we come to open our corolla in the world. We have come only to wilt. Let your bitterness cease for a moment: even for a moment let us cast away sorrow! What shall we sing, oh my friends? In what shall we delight?"[53]

This subunit ends by encouraging readers to take action wherever they can (9:10). We must make use of the vital energy of our bodies. But we must do it ourselves, not as an imposition of enslavement to the economic production demanded by the Ptolemaic empire; not even for ourselves if it does not give the pleasure of enjoying life. The reason for acting now is that we know about the infallible coming of death. In death there is no vital energy, in physical power or in knowledge. Reason, knowledge, and wisdom are the preferred activities of the wise. Therefore Qoheleth affirms that in spite of the misery of the present, "a living dog is better than a dead lion" (9:4).

Qoheleth's invitation is not to suicide, cynicism, or resignation; it is rather to affirm material and relational life, where we can feel the palpitations of the heart. It is to enjoy, share, and work without complexity or anxiety: with purity of heart.

The Race Is Not Always to the Swift (9:11-12)

[11]Again I saw that under the sun the race is not to the swift, nor the battle to the strong, nor bread to the wise, nor riches to the intelligent, nor favor to the skillful; but time and chance happen to them all. [12]For no one can anticipate the time of disaster. Like fish taken in a cruel net, and like

*birds caught in a snare, so mortals are snared at a time of
calamity, when it suddenly falls upon them.*

Continuing the previous reflection, we must recognize that
good people do not always get the best results in an inverted
society. Even when athletes, heroes, or sages put all their effort
into winning, or into getting what they want, they do not
always achieve it. Others use influence, luck, or manipulation to
rob them of the victory they deserve. Therefore we should not
lose heart when our expectations are not fulfilled.

Verse 12 brings in echoes of 3:1 and 10. Here Qoheleth is
referring to the time of death, misfortune, or calamity. They are
unforeseen. His metaphors of a fish in the net or a bird in a
snare are poignant. Indeed, it is totally frustrating to fall unex-
pectedly into a mortal trap, when we have our life ahead of us.
That is why Qoheleth insists so much on learning to live life in
human dignity, and with all the necessary realism. That is, without forgetting that death, or any calamity, may appear at any
moment. That should not cause us anguish or premature death.
To know that we will die someday, as everyone does, helps us to
seek life and accept it maturely, in order to enjoy its fullness . . .
as much as possible.

WISDOM IN TIMES OF "SAVE YOUR
OWN SKIN" (9:13-11:6)

This unit consists of a series of maxims for survival in difficult
times, when the horizons seem to be closing in and the theme of
the day is "save your own skin." Qoheleth advocates taking
things as they come, with great serenity, maturity, and above all,
wisdom. Wisdom is seldom respected when it comes from those
who are poor and socially insignificant. But he knows from
experience that wisdom is powerful when it is well used (9:13-
18). Therefore we must walk with wisdom through the day-to-
day struggle for survival, carefully choosing our actions
(10:8-11) and our words (10:12-15). We must work when

there is work to do, and enjoy a banquet when we can, discerning the time for work and the time for rest. We must not speak in haste against the authorities, because that can be fatal (10:20). We must be always alert and try to read the signs of the times (11:1-5). Since we don't know when or how the situation will change, we must keep on working and be ready for anything: "It's better to be safe than sorry."

The Power of Wisdom (9:13-18)

> ¹³*I have also seen this example of wisdom under the sun, and it seemed great to me.* ¹⁴*There was a little city with few people in it. A great king came against it and besieged it, building great siegeworks against it.* ¹⁵*Now there was found in it a poor wise man, and he by his wisdom delivered the city. Yet no one remembered that poor man.* ¹⁶*So I said, "Wisdom is better than might; yet the poor man's wisdom is despised, and his words are not heeded."*
> ¹⁷*The quiet words of the wise are more to be heeded*
> *than the shouting of a ruler among fools.*
> ¹⁸*Wisdom is better than weapons of war,*
> *but one bungler destroys much good.*

Here Qoheleth inserts a narrative type of wisdom teaching (9:13-16) into the series of proverbs that make up the unit. The hero of the parable, the liberator of a small city, is a wise man in humble circumstances; his tale echoes that of the poor youth in 4:13. This narrative uses several contrasts to emphasize that wisdom is more powerful than other forces. The city is small in size and population, and it is mightily besieged by a powerful king. There is no power capable of meeting this invading force. No one sees a way of escaping total defeat by the conqueror. But the poor wise man, against all expectations, uses his wisdom to liberate the city. The narrator doesn't tell us how; he only says it was done by a poor wise man. This great, unexpected historical event reminds us of the exodus, or of David's triumph over Goliath. The problem that Qoheleth sees is that the hero of such a great event was forgotten, because he was poor.

This is Qoheleth's reproach to the collective conscience of the people. They have forgotten that with wisdom, they can find ways out of an apparently impossible situation. And they look down on the poor, even when the poor are wise; rather they listen to the rich, even those who speak foolishness. In his conclusion to the parable ("So I said . . ."), Qoheleth exhorts his readers to be guided by the power of wisdom and not by might. The poor must believe in the poor who are wise, and not despise their wisdom.

Some versions translate the verb "liberate" (*millat*) in the future conditional tense: he might have delivered the city. Both are possible in the Hebrew. The future conditional would carry the same connotations, but with more emphasis on the people's disregard for the poor wise man. The city was defeated because its inhabitants didn't ask for his advice; that attitude showed their disregard for wisdom. In a "save-your-own-skin" situation, wisdom should enlighten our behavior and survival. Even though defeat was clearly predictable in the face of such an extreme imbalance of power (9:14), there might have been a way out (9:15).

Verses 17-18 continue the allusion to wisdom, including not only its power but also its vulnerability. Verse 17 draws a contrast between quiet words and shouting. Quiet words are well thought out, a mark of the wise; but fools prefer the shouting of the people in power. That attitude will only lead to failure, the narrator warns.

In v. 18 Qoheleth makes his description of wisdom more precise. The first part repeats more emphatically what he has already said: that wisdom is better than weapons. But, he adds, a small mistake or error[54] (in the application of wisdom) can be fatal; it destroys much of the good that was achieved. The same idea is repeated in 10:1, 11.

Calm in the Face of Madness (10:1-7)

> 10¹ *Dead flies make the perfumer's ointment give off a*
> *foul odor;*
> *so a little folly outweighs wisdom and honor.*
> ² *The heart of the wise inclines to the right,*
> *but the heart of a fool to the left.*
> ³ *Even when fools walk on the road, they lack sense,*
> *and show to everyone that they are fools.*
> ⁴ *If the anger of the ruler rises against you, do not leave*
> *your post,*
> *for calmness will undo great offenses.*
> ⁵ *There is an evil that I have seen under the sun, as great*
> *an error as if it proceeded from the ruler:* ⁶ *folly is set in many*
> *high places, and the rich sit in a low place.* ⁷ *I have seen slaves*
> *on horseback, and princes walking on foot like slaves.*

In this fragment Qoheleth shows his readers the importance of knowing how to behave in adverse situations, produced by a society where things go well for the wicked and badly for the righteous. He warns against making simple mistakes, because although wisdom is more powerful than might, not to act wisely can be fatal. Here Qoheleth compares foolishness with wisdom and recognizes that no matter how hard people try, a little foolishness can ruin even their best efforts. In 10:1 he quotes a well-known proverb, which conveys that meaning despite its difficult construction in Hebrew. Just as a fly can contaminate perfume made by an expert, so a pinch of folly can ruin the reputation of a wise man.[55]

Verse 2 draws the contrast between the wise and the foolish. The wise work for good, and fools for wickedness (cf. 2:14). Fools cannot hide their folly (10:3); it shows in their way of speaking and acting. The second part of this verse is ambiguous.* It may mean "he says of everyone, this is a fool"; or, "he

---

* The Spanish version used by the author renders v. 3b as follows: "and he goes around saying to everyone that he is a fool."

says to everyone that he is a fool."[56] The ambiguity is appropriate, since it is a mark of foolishness to call someone else a fool.

Verse 4 again introduces the unpleasant ruler, probably the same one referred to in 8:9. Qoheleth's advice focuses on the survival of those who are close to the king. They must wisely keep calm in the face of the sovereign's anger. One false move can be fatal. One should not leave the king's presence hastily, because it may be interpreted as rebellion and in despotic times one must know how to avoid premature death.

Verses 5-7 reflect the order of Qoheleth's world: the authorities are set up to do good and administer justice. What happens under the sun, which he sees as a calamity, is that inept and corrupt people are placed in important leadership positions, while those who are competent to hold those positions,[57] people of noble origin, have been pushed aside. Qoheleth surely has in mind the rulers of Greek origin who were put in power without regard to their ability, displacing the rich, noble Jewish families.[58]

Verse 7 is a picture of disorder from Qoheleth's viewpoint. As an aristocrat he finds it distasteful that inept bureaucrats of dubious origin are put in power; it is as if a servant, who would normally walk, rode horseback while the princes walked on foot. This metaphor, perhaps from a proverb of his time, indicates the invertedness of things in comparison with what would be considered normal. He is probably affirming that those who happen to be in power—that is, the Ptolemaic officials and other Jews of dubious origin, should not be there.

In the view of José Vílchez Lindez, it is a picture of "a reversed world." Qoheleth is speaking as a prophet, says Vílchez, "pointing his finger at one of the worst flaws of the society: the ineptitude of the rulers, for which the top authorities are responsible."[59]

Choon-Leong Seow connects this fragment with the one that follows. That is interesting, because it would be interpreted as a comment on the instability of the new social order, in which unexpected things may happen. At the macro level, says Seow, "a society in transition can be dangerous: social, economic, and political forces can bring unexpected changes, in the midst of which one may become a victim."[60]

Watch Your Step! (10:8-11)

> [8] *Whoever digs a pit will fall into it;*
> *and whoever breaks through a wall will be bitten by*
> *a snake.*
> [9] *Whoever quarries stones will be hurt by them;*
> *and whoever splits logs will be endangered by them.*
> [10] *If the iron is blunt, and one does not whet the edge,*
> *then more strength must be exerted;*
> *but wisdom helps one to succeed.*
> [11] *If the snake bites before it is charmed,*
> *there is no advantage in a charmer.*

This fragment is held together by the theme of constant risk in everyday life. The risks are greater in a "save-your-own-skin" society; one must be careful about even the smallest details in order not to get hurt. Everything must be done with care and wisdom. This is the way to defend life against the risks we impose on ourselves in working or in making decisions.

The first two verses have a similar structure. They may refer in general to everyday risks at work, but they can also be read figuratively as a warning to those who decide to undertake an action. Such people must know the dangers and consequences the action may entail.

The other two verses complete the advice. If our knives, scythes, or sickles are not sharp, we will have to use more strength. If our tools are in good condition, the work is lighter, more efficient, and of better quality. The metaphor applies equally to everyday acts and to strategic choices. Human life is the most important thing; to preserve it we must use wisdom in agricultural or urban labor. Overconfidence is dangerous; if you carelessly put your hand into the stones, a snake may bite you.[61]

Thus in 10:8-11 we see three important warnings: (1) One must recognize the dangers in the actions one is involved in, and always be alert. (2) One must use the right tools—whether they are objects or methods—for each action. This means always applying wisdom, since it guarantees efficiency and survival. (3) Finally, Qoheleth insists on staying alert right up to the end. If we work with zeal but get careless for a moment, the whole project may be ruined. Snake-charming skills are of no use if the snake bites the charmer in a moment of carelessness.[62] This verse continues the warning of 9:18 and 10:1.

Watch What You Say! (10:12-15)

> [12] *Words spoken by the wise bring them favor,*
> *but the lips of fools consume them.*
> [13] *The words of their mouths begin in foolishness,*
> *and their talk ends in wicked madness;*
> [14] *yet fools talk on and on.*
> *No one knows what is to happen,*
> *and who can tell anyone what the future holds?*
> [15] *The toil of fools wears them out,*
> *for they do not even know the way to town.*

Now Qoheleth returns to the importance of words and declarations. He spoke of them earlier, in 4:17-5:6 [Heb. 5:1-7]. Here he brings in some well-known, traditional proverbs. We can read them in the context of the "save-your-own-skin" society.

To the wise, the use of words is a fundamental key to survival. Verses 12-14 emphasize the way fools use words, in contrast to the way of the wise. While the words of the wise are generally accepted as enlightening, those of fools are not only repugnant (for their lack of wisdom) but also dangerous; they can bring the speaker to a quick end. Qoheleth's readers must try to follow the example of the wise and be very careful what they say. Careless affirmations can have mortal consequences.

Verse 13 pursues his description of fools' words. They not only say silly things but progressively[63] introduce new stupidities and end up raving madly. One must avoid being like them and also protect oneself from them. They are recognizable because they talk too much and without foundation, and they talk about things they do not know, such as the future. Qoheleth has said this several times (cf. 6:12; 7:14; 8:7). As a sage, he does not know what is to come, and that lack of knowledge is very painful to him. The fool does not recognize the impossibility of seeing the next horizons, beyond death. Perhaps Qoheleth is saying that we should not get involved in complex or unmanageable issues, as fools do. To survive in anti-human situations we must keep our feet on the ground, in real life.

Verse 15 is a proverbial phrase of difficult translation. The *Jerusalem Bible* renders it: "What bothers the fool most is that he does not know how to go to the city." Robert Michaud says, following Norbert Lohfink's translation: "Toil wears out the fool; no one has shown him the way to the city." Ravasi suggests that fools "take the wrong road to the city and thus they get lost, worn out with fatigue."

Apparently the problem is in fitting the two affirmations (vv. 15a and 15b) together. It may be either a proverb we don't know or a statement of the obvious: it is easy to go to the city—everyone knows the way, but fools can't do even that. The first part of the verse refers to labor (ʿamal). In the wisdom tradition, fools are known for their laziness. But for Qoheleth it is not just their laziness but a lack of intelligence in their work that makes them tiresome and boring. Today we would say, "they just don't get it." The first part of the verse could also be expressed in another saying: "the lazy have to work twice as hard." That is, they don't get it right and have to do it over. Even then it doesn't work, because "those who are born to be tamales, think the leaves fall from heaven" ("Once a fool, always a fool"). By describing the behavior of fools, Qoheleth is advising his readers not to become one. In a "save-your-own-skin" society, foolishness aggravates failure and leads to total frustration.

For Michaud, going to the city is a metaphor for getting rich or climbing the social ladder. In this case it would mean that fools work to exhaustion and still don't know how to get rich or get ahead. The reading would be: "What bothers the fool most is not knowing how to get rich."

In my view the simplest interpretation of the text is that fools don't know anything at all. Since they don't even know the way to the city, it is hard for them to survive and defend themselves in their rapacious society.

Careful! The Walls Have Ears (10:16-20)

> ¹⁶ *Alas for you, O land, when your king is a servant,*
>   *and your princes feast in the morning!*
> ¹⁷ *Happy are you, O land, when your king is a noble man,*
>   *and your princes feast at the proper time—*
>   *for strength, and not for drunkenness!*
> ¹⁸ *Through sloth the roof sinks in,*
>   *and through indolence the house leaks.*
> ¹⁹ *Feasts are made for laughter;*
>   *wine gladdens life,*
>   *and money meets every need.*
> ²⁰ *Do not curse the king, even in your thoughts,*
>   *or curse the rich, even in your bedroom;*
>   *for a bird of the air may carry your voice,*
>   *or some winged creature tell the matter.*

This fragment criticizes the lifestyle of the rulers in an inverted society. Qoheleth has already challenged the officials who do not administer justice (3:16; 8:11), who are corrupt and inefficient (5:8 [Heb. 5:7]; 8:10; 10:5), and the sovereigns who are despotic toward their people and their subjects (8:2-4; 10:4). Now he addresses their everyday behavior (vv. 16-17).

He compares two types of sovereigns: those who do not attend to the needs of their people or are ill-prepared to defend their nation against invasion, and those who take responsibility as they should. He uses the metaphors of gluttony, feasting, and partying to draw the contrast. Sovereigns who cannot move their kingdom forward do not control their officials. Their horizon is irresponsible entertainment. The text uses the word *na⁽ar* to describe these sovereigns. *Na⁽ar* can mean a child or youth, or alternatively, a servant. Servant makes a better contrast with the sovereign in v. 17, who is described as a free man (ranking citizen), of noble birth. Qoheleth may be continuing the theme of 10:5, where he sees it as calamitous that inept people of dubious origin are elevated to positions of great dignity. Then v. 16 would support his description of the negligent behavior of the princes. But *na⁽ar* can also mean a child, suggesting their inability to control their officials, who abusively take advantage of the situation.

The prophets strongly criticized the behavior of feasting and drunkenness in the morning (Isaiah 5:11; 5:22; Amos 6:4-6). The verb "to feast" is in the imperfect tense, suggesting frequent repetition.[64]

As we have clearly seen elsewhere in the book, Qoheleth is not against feasting and enjoyment; on the contrary, he proposes it as an alternative in his miserable society. But we can deduce that his society has reached a state of total frustration, precisely because the rulers have not taken their responsibility as they should: they are corrupt, despotic, unjust, oppressive, and devoted to personal entertainment. Verse 18, a well-known refrain describing the disastrous consequences of laziness, may refer to the failure of the royal administration caused by its inattention to the proper business of the state. According to Michaud, the Egyptian royal ideology (adopted by the Ptolemies) related "the house" to "the state": "The king manages affairs of state, as the homeowner rules his house. The country belongs to him."[65]

The responsible, wise[66] sovereign knows how to discern the right times and purposes for eating and drinking. He is alert and attentive to his responsibilities toward his people.

From Qoheleth's comparison between the two types of leaders, we see his yearning for a king who knows how to manage his kingdom. The "save-your-own-skin" society is the result of its rulers' inability to reorder their society in a just and humane way, which is their true task.

Verse 19 is related to v. 16. As Maillot says, this is not a brief moment of jubilation but a description of the court drunkards.[67] The key word in this passage is "money." The princes can behave as they do, devoting themselves to feasting and drunkenness, because they have money. Money is the answer to everything; it can deflect criticism and buy people's loyalty. As we say, "money can make even dogs dance."

Verse 20 follows this rereading perfectly. Qoheleth is criticizing the irresponsible rulers, but he reminds his readers that it is dangerous to speak ill of those who hold power in their hands. Thus, in times of acute repression, he warns against conspiring or speaking ill of the king, the rich, or "important men."[68]

The danger is that somehow—through spies, informers, or domestic servants—the people in power will find out and react with mortal repression. One must survive; that means to be shrewd in everything and to avoid doing or saying anything about dangerous matters. "The walls have ears" is our way of saying that a little bird may pass on what we have said. Take care, says Qoheleth; there are spies in the most unexpected places, even in your own house and bedroom.

Better to Be Safe Than Sorry (11:1-6)

> 11[1] *Send out your bread upon the waters,*
> *for after many days you will get it back.*
> [2] *Divide your means seven ways, or even eight,*
> *for you do not know what disaster may happen on earth.*
> [3] *When clouds are full,*
> *they empty rain on the earth;*
> *whether a tree falls to the south or to the north,*
> *in the place where the tree falls, there it will lie.*
> [4] *Whoever observes the wind will not sow;*
> *and whoever regards the clouds will not reap.*
> [5] *Just as you do not know how the breath comes to the bones in the mother's womb, so you do not know the work of God, who makes everything.*

> *⁶In the morning sow your seed, and at evening do not let your hands be idle; for you do not know which will prosper, this or that, or whether both alike will be good.*

Here is more advice about surviving in times of total frustration. This fragment opens and closes with imperatives for action. It is a challenge to discern the proper times (3:1-8, 17; 8:6) for moving ahead. Qoheleth recommends taking risks and also sharing. It must all be done with wisdom, but in the recognition that we will never fully understand events under the sun. There is a mystery in God's work that is beyond human understanding. Since we do not know the future, and since we see it as possibly threatening (v. 2), we must hedge our bets in order to survive.

Verses 1 and 2 are of like structure, although they seem to carry conflicting meanings. "Send out your bread upon the waters" is an ancient proverb and has been interpreted in different ways. Some commentators think it is about maritime investments, for future profit. They see v. 2a as a diversification of investments, to protect against failures that can lead to total loss. This reading may be valid in the context of the feverish commercial activity of Qoheleth's time.

However, I prefer to take it in terms of sharing.⁶⁹ Qoheleth does not recommend the accumulation of wealth. Verse 1 points to a broader meaning, about taking risks in whatever one does, in the expectation that in time it will be worthwhile; the reward will come. Verse 2 would then mean sharing or giving generously. The reason for these imperatives is that no one can know the future; why is everyone so concerned about profit? The situation seems unlikely to improve. Since the horizon is impenetrable to the human eye, we have to live in the present; and since the medium-range future is not promising, we have to live dangerously in the present—placing our bets on the side of good, distributing generously. Let us remember that Qoheleth is against the accumulation of money or goods.

Verses 3 and 4, informed by nature (clouds, rain, a tree, the wind), show that we can predict certain short-term events deductively, from our suspicions. There is regularity in the signs of nature: when the clouds are full, it will rain. Where the tree falls, it stays. The regularity is obvious. In other words, although Qoheleth's world is full of uncertainty, there are discernible clues that people can use to guide their everyday practice. Even so, we still have to take risks. Verse 4 points out that too much prudence can paralyze all action. If we study the wind too much, we will never sow; the same thing happens if we spend all our time watching the clouds. In short, we have to discern the right times, applying all the necessary wisdom but also taking the necessary risks.

In any case, Qoheleth insists, human beings cannot understand all the mysteries that happen under the sun. He has said that often, and he repeats it here. Recognizing our limitations is a part of wisdom. Verse 5 describes our human inability to understand the mystery of life in a mother's womb.[70] It is a work of God, a mystery. Sometimes we do everything with sufficient discernment and wisdom, but the final results may be different. We do not always get what we expect.

This unit of reflection ends with an imperative to action. Qoheleth uses an agricultural metaphor: sow your seed without ceasing, morning and evening, in order to avoid possible failure. Again his reason is that we do not know the future; no one does, in a "save-your-own-skin" society.

LIVING LIFE IN HAPPINESS AND DIGNITY . . . BEFORE WE GO TO THE GRAVE (11:7-12:7)

The final part of the final section describes Qoheleth's proposal, which he has mentioned here and there in the overall discourse, with greater clarity and breadth. His proposal is to live life as it is, straightforwardly, as a way of resisting the globalizing frustration produced by his soulless society. Light, joy, pleasure, enjoyment, and good humor are the indispensable ingredients we need to savor life with intensity, here and now. This is an urgent warning not to let death—from total frustration—come prematurely and wreak havoc in a "save-your-own-skin" society. Physical death will come, inevitably; it is part of human nature. That is why we should make as much as we can of life, as well as we can. Here he is speaking especially to the young, for they have the best chances of moving forward. Their life is not too complicated by laws and institutions; they are better able to take risks. Qoheleth calls them to enjoy life before it is too late; before the cosmos darkens, before the social decadence becomes irreversible, before death arrives. They must affirm life now, so that death will not come before its time.

Live Intensely in the Present . . . the Days of Darkness Are Infinite (11:7-8)

> *⁷ Light is sweet, and it is pleasant for the eyes to see the sun.*
> *⁸ Even those who live many years should rejoice in them all; yet let them remember that the days of darkness will be many. All that comes is vanity.*

Verse 7 opens the final song of the book. It invites us to live in spite of the situation of total frustration, because life is better than death. The parallel synonyms of v. 7 highlight this point. It is sweet—pleasant—to see the light—the sun. Qoheleth is also combining the sense of sight (the light) with that of taste (sweetness).[71]

To see the sun means to be alive, to live (cf. 6:5).[72] Life is light, in spite of the disappointment of the present "under the sun." Light has always had a deep symbolic value. It is joy, happiness, fullness; to see and feel the heat of the sun means to live.[73]

"Rejoice in" or "enjoy" (*samah*) and "remember" (*zakar*) are the key words in the poem.[74] They appear in this first fragment and are repeated in the next two. Qoheleth recommends enjoying—now—all the years of our life. His reason is that old age and death are the unavoidable future for everyone. Shadows and darkness are symbols of death.

Since the future, the past, and the present are all *hebel,* Qoheleth sees enjoying the present as the only way to counteract the absurd world that leads to total disillusionment. If old age and death are empty and inevitable realities, we can still counteract the absurd present and its frustrations. This can only be done by affirming everyday humanity, through joy wherever we find it. The act of remembering the coming annoyances of old age, dying, and death, underlines the urgency of seeking enjoyment in life today. Here rejoicing is a way of struggling for life, under siege from the frustrating present and from the imminence of death.

Live Joyfully and without Anxiety . . .
but Wisely (11:9-10)

> *⁹Rejoice, young man, while you are young, and let your heart cheer you in the days of your youth. Follow the inclination of your heart and the desire of your eyes, but know that for all these things God will bring you into judgment.*
> *¹⁰Banish anxiety from your mind, and put away pain from your body; for youth and the dawn of life are vanity.*

Here Qoheleth intensifies the vehemence of his invitation to enjoy life. Now he is addressing the young, in the second person imperative. In the last fragment he was speaking in the third person, to human beings in general—young or old—and in terms short of the imperative.[75] This may be because he is addressing youth, adolescents,[76] at a stage of life that passes quickly. Vílchez says that here his discourse conveys a sense of urgency because time is running out, it doesn't stop, and we can never get it back.[77] Qoheleth describes youth as *hebel;* this is one of the few places in the book where *hebel* does not mean absurd, but fleeting or ephemeral. But we can also see frustration in his recognition that youth, the fullness of life, is like a puff of wind.

Verse 9 advises the readers affirmatively on the search for

happiness. They should follow the inclination of the heart and the desire of the eyes, the internal and the external. Qoheleth is calling for full freedom to seek happiness especially when one is young, daring, and not imprisoned by norms. In Hebrew thought, says Ravasi, happiness lies above all in physical enjoyment: eating, drinking, and entertainment.[78]

As usual, Qoheleth's advice goes against tradition. The Hebrew Bible recommends against giving free rein to the desires of the heart (Isaiah 57:17; Numbers 15:39; Job 31:7).

As I said earlier, the last part of v. 9 is a later addition by a pious hand, intending to moderate Qoheleth's advice. But as Vittoria D'Alario points out, it is not out of line with the author's own dialectical and oppositional thinking.[79] Others see the call to judgment as a rendering of accounts to God, that one has not taken advantage of the gift of life. Reading the text in the context of a "save-your-own-skin" society, the call to do everything conscientiously is important. Qoheleth does not want to reinforce the individualism promoted by his society. His advice to seek full happiness may be misunderstood. Here the call to happiness is a call to be human, to feel one's body in an inhuman society; it is part of the struggle to survive with dignity. For that reason it is crucial to remember that to seek one's own happiness should not mean trampling one another or making others suffer. The call to judgment means that God sets limits, not in the sense of asceticism but in defense of everyone's happiness. To fear God, as we saw earlier, also means recognizing one's own limitations in order not to victimize others.

Verse 10 discusses the search for happiness by a negative line of reasoning. We must try hard to avoid anxiety, which leads to unhappiness, and not allow the body (flesh) to suffer. A healthy mind (heart) and a healthy body make possible the joy of living. For Qoheleth, youth offers real possibilities of counteracting the deadly logic of his society. It is as if Qoheleth, in nostalgic tones, is telling his students that they have a different power and should use it now; they should not be suffocated by the opaque horizons they see in the old age of the people around them.

Remember the God of Life in Your Good Days . . .
before Death Comes (12:1-7)

> *12¹Remember your creator in the days of your youth, before the days of trouble come, and the years draw near when you will say, "I have no pleasure in them"; ²before the sun and the light and the moon and the stars are darkened and the clouds return with the rain; ³in the day when the guards of the house tremble, and the strong men are bent, and the women who grind cease working because they are few, and those who look through the windows see dimly; ⁴when the doors on the street are shut, and the sound of the grinding is low, and one rises up at the sound of a bird, and all the daughters of song are brought low; ⁵when one is afraid of heights, and terrors are in the road; the almond tree blossoms, the grasshopper drags itself along and desire fails; because all must go to their eternal home, and the mourners will go about the streets; ⁶before the silver cord is snapped, and the golden bowl is broken, and the pitcher is broken at the fountain, and the wheel broken at the cistern, ⁷and the dust returns to the earth as it was, and the breath returns to God who gave it.*

This poem, one of Qoheleth's most beautiful, has been interpreted in different ways. Many people see it as an allegory on old age; others, as a euphemism for physical death. I see in it an allusion to total decadence: in the cosmos, in society, and in humanity. It is like a three-dimensional poem, using old age as a metaphor for brokenness.

But the emphasis is not on decadence and death, although the author devotes most of the verses to them. The emphasis is on the imperative to remember the Creator now, before it is too late to do something in life that will fully please God.

The poem opens with a reference to the Creator,[80] that is, God the giver of life; and closes with the return of the breath of life to God who gave it. Life is loaned by God; that is why the spirit returns to God. The imperative "Remember your

Creator" is connected to the earlier imperative, "Rejoice" or "enjoy." By their equivalent position we see God as the meaning of life and joy and vice versa: in joy we see the presence of God. Qoheleth's exhortation is to live life, the presence of God, joyfully, before it is too late. In this sense, the allusion to God is the theological basis for enjoyment and joy.[81]

There is a similar connection between "Remember" in 12:1 and in 11:8. In 11:8 it reminds us of death in order to intensify the invitation to enjoy life now, in view of eternal death. In 12:1, by its chiastic placement, Qoheleth invites us to remember the giver of life now, before death comes.

There is also a connection between the Creator in 12:1 and the God who will judge acts (11:9) under the sun; this is the third reference to God in this unit. The text should not be interpreted moralistically, to diminish the call to enjoy life. It is about the just God who hears the cry of the victims, even though in 4:1 God seems to be absent from Qoheleth's society. The call is to his readers, to move forward in the struggle for survival. They must remember God and make God present. The God who judges is the one who establishes limits for the defense of all creatures. It is the Creator who gives life to everyone. We must hold on to this God before death comes, in a decadent society that smells of death.

Following the imperative "Remember your Creator," there are three moments marked by the word "before . . ." (ʿad ʾasher). The first (12:1b) announces the days of trouble, described in vv. 2-7; these are the days in which human beings, despite all their wishes, cannot achieve human fulfillment. There is no springtime habitat for them, no joy in the community of a household. Qoheleth uses the metaphor of old age, with its weaknesses and lack of vitality. The second "before" opens the description of the days of trouble: the end of the cosmos (12:2), of the people (12:3-4), and of humanity. The third "before" describes death (vv. 6-7).

In v. 2 the sun, the moon, and the stars—that is, day and night—are turned into eternal darkness. Nature is paralyzed in a dark winter. After the rain, the blue sky never returns.

Verses 3-4 describe the gradual decadence of society; Qoheleth uses the metaphor of a house or palace, melancholically describing its ruined state.[82] Verse 3 is devoted to its inhabitants. Nothing is left of the gallantry and bravery of its guards. There are no more banquet preparations: few women are grinding food, few guests are eating. The women, who give life to a household, no longer see through the windows; like the sun, moon, and stars, the house too is dark. There is nothing to admire in the time of death. Verse 4 describes the interior of the house. The doors to the street are shut. There is a sepulchral silence. Visitors do not come in, and no one goes out into the street. The cosmos and the household are united only by silence and darkness. The sound of the mill fades away, and so does the song of the bird. That is why, before all the songs fall silent, we must enjoy life and hold on to the Giver of life.

Verse 5 describes the old age of human beings. It stands in opposition to youth, as described in 11:9-10. In place of boldness, there is fear. "The almond tree blossoms" may mean the appearance of grey hairs.[83] The elderly walk with a heavy gait, dragging their feet like the grasshopper. Caper berries, known for their digestive and aphrodisiac qualities, lose their effects. The desire to eat abundantly and to make love is dissipated. The funeral preparations are ready. The eternal home is death, *sheol;* the funeral cortege of mourners is already in the streets.

The third "before" (12:6-7) describes death. Verse 6 is a beautiful euphemism for death.[84] The four synonymous verbs used here connote destruction. The golden ball, bowl, or cup has been interpreted as a lamp hung from a silver cord; both are destroyed, leaving absolute darkness. In the same way the pitcher of water, the source of life, is broken and the pulley wheel,[85] which lifts the pitcher, is destroyed and sunk in the well. The well may be the same as a tomb.

Verse 7 is a nonmetaphorical description of death. It echoes the origin of the creation of human beings (Genesis 3:20). Human beings return to nothingness.

With this gloomy picture of society, the city, the house, or old age, Qoheleth makes very clear his pessimistic vision of the future. His horizons are closed. In his moment of history he cannot find the energy of a light pointing to any real change in social conditions. For Qoheleth, the future lies in taking on the present in a different way. He thinks we should not hope to celebrate life in the future. It must be done now, in the midst of the frustration of the present, and with the energy of a youthful body and heart. The future must be lived now. Death will come in its time. There is a time for everything. Death must not be hastened, nor should the decadence of the frustrating society invade the present.

Epilogues

The book ends with three epilogues by different authors.[1]

The first epilogue (12:8) embraces the whole book. It consists of the same phrase that was introduced in 1:2. Some say that it is not from Qoheleth's hand but from that of a student of his. In fact it fits the whole meaning of the book, and we cannot discard the possibility that Qoheleth himself put it there.

The second (12:9-11) presents a profile of Qoheleth by a disciple who venerated the teacher or by a friendly colleague. Its purpose is to recommend the teacher's wisdom.

The third epilogue (12:12-14) is said to be an addition designed to moderate Qoheleth's thought, which was unorthodox by traditional standards.

TOTAL FRUSTRATION (12:8)

8 Vanity of vanities, says the Teacher; all is vanity.

Whether or not it is Qoheleth's, this verse reflects the narrator's vision. Qoheleth is a renegade sage, in opposition to his present society. The phrase shows all the anger aroused in him by the works of those who rule his upside-down world. At the end of his book, Qoheleth has not changed his mind about the present time in which he lives. But the phrase should not be read in the same way as at the beginning. Now it reflects a whole journey through the hard life of Qoheleth's world. The "save-your-own-skin" society generates immense frustration in everyone. Recognizing that frustration, Qoheleth says thirty-eight times that it is *hebel*. Nevertheless, he invites us to survive with dignity, to search for a new logic of life that will lead to human fulfillment. This is only possible if we hold on to life in the present, in the midst of total frustration. The wisdom he offers is intended to help his readers learn to live with dignity in the most discouraging situations of life in the present, past, and future.

PRESENTATION OF THE NARRATOR (12:9-11)

⁹Besides being wise, the Teacher also taught the people knowledge, weighing and studying and arranging many proverbs. ¹⁰The Teacher sought to find pleasing words, and he wrote words of truth plainly.

¹¹The sayings of the wise are like goads, and like nails firmly fixed are the collected sayings that are given by one shepherd.

These three verses represent a recommendation of the author of the book of Qoheleth. It is full of praise; perhaps such a controversial writing had caused great disturbance in his milieu, leading the disciple or colleague to see a need to bolster the circulation of the book. The author of this epilogue agrees with Qoheleth's thinking and intends, with this recommendation, that it be taken seriously.

He says nothing to identify Qoheleth with Solomon (1:12-2:26); he simply presents him as a wise man who pursued his investigation conscientiously. Qoheleth was a teacher of the whole people, not only of students from the privileged sector. Perhaps he gave classes to a select group of students, and at the same time spread his words of wisdom in the plazas and streets, as was the custom of roving philosophers in the Hellenistic period.[2] Besides investigating and discerning realities, he was also a prolific composer of proverbs: sentences of truth and beauty. The author of the epilogue emphasizes the combination of elegance and truth (v. 10).

Verse 11 closes the second epilogue by describing the purpose of words of wisdom. He uses pastoral and agricultural metaphors. Wise words have the same purpose as the goads or spurs used to direct beasts of burden and make them walk; or they are like stakes to hold a tent securely against the wind or rain.[3] Some people say that the shepherd mentioned here is a reference to God as the source of the sages' wisdom. If so, the author of this epilogue is suggesting that Qoheleth's words come from God.

TOO MUCH STUDYING IS BAD FOR THE HEALTH (12:12-14)

[12]*Of anything beyond these, my child, beware. Of making many books there is no end, and much study is a weariness of the flesh.*

[13]*The end of the matter; all has been heard. Fear God, and keep his commandments; for that is the whole duty of everyone.* [14]*For God will bring every deed into judgment, including every secret thing, whether good or evil.*

Commentators believe that this epilogue is later than the preceding one. Most believe that it is radically different from Qoheleth's thought. The author is conservative and is trying to give the book an interpretive key more in line with the orthodox wisdom tradition. It may have been added in the period when teaching was being reformed (200 B.C.E., after the conquest of Antiochus III), for the purpose of warning youth against Hellenistic influence—not as Qoheleth did, which seemed a dangerous way, but by means of tradition.[4] The thinking of the epilogue's author is in line with that of Ben Sirach, who combines the fear of God with the act of keeping the commandments (Sirach 1:26-28; 2:15-16).

The phrase "my child," characteristic of that tradition, appears in the book of Proverbs. Qoheleth does not use it. In v. 12 we can see the polemic that may have led to Qoheleth's writing, as it led to so many philosophical positions in his time. The author of the epilogue is not against studying or against books but rather against the endless theoretical discussions that lead to nothing good but only to alienation from reality. Perhaps he is trying to avoid the consumeristic search for the newest and latest ideas.

The author is pragmatic; he sees it as risky to let Qoheleth's book circulate in its current form, reinforced by the recommendation that appears in vv. 9-11. So at the end he adds three things that readers should keep in mind when they read the book, to guard against the confusion of a world convulsed by the penetration of the dominant Hellenistic culture. The three themes are the fear of God, keeping the commandments, and a reminder that God will judge both visible and secret, good and evil acts.

This writer's approach to the three themes is different from Qoheleth's. Here the fear of God is not a recognition of human limitations in the work of transforming the world, which turns human beings into true subjects. For the author of the epilogue the fear of God goes with obedience to the commandments, an attitude that Qoheleth ignores throughout his discourse. It is contrary to Qoheleth's attitude, because human beings do not become subjects by following the law, but by affirming life with trust in God's grace.

Verse 14 picks up the theme of judgment that Qoheleth also used (11:6), but in a different way. The author of the epilogue relates judgment to obeying the law.[5] In the context of the time, he was probably referring to judgment after death. In Qoheleth there is nothing after death. All judgment takes place under the sun. For Qoheleth it is true that everything is in God's hands: the righteous, the wise, and their works, but he has no assurance that justice will triumph over the wickedness that happens under the sun. The author of the epilogue seeks to infuse that assurance into a world filled with uncertainty.

It is up to the reader to evaluate and discern the purposes of these two authors.

Conclusion

Obviously the reading of Qoheleth presented here has been done in the context of our present reality, with the globalization of the free market. But there is an extraordinary similarity between those Hellenistic times and our own. Therefore there is no need to draw a separate application for our own times. The reader has probably been doing that throughout this book.

To summarize, Qoheleth recommends four ways of resisting frustration in a present whose horizons are closed. First, by affirming the faith that there is a time and a season for everything; that is, at some point the horizons will have to open up. Second, by affirming real life, now, as a rhythm of life in opposition to the rhythm of a society that has no interest in human beings. Third, the fear of God as a recognition of the human condition, finite and limited in what it can do. And fourth, the attitude of discernment and wisdom in the everyday tasks of the "meanwhile," in a society whose ideology seems to be "save your own skin!" Thus it offers plenty of advice for surviving and avoiding premature death. It also recommends solidarity: "two are better than one," because "a threefold cord does not break."

The question remains: Is embracing the present sufficient for human fulfillment in our world today? Doesn't it lead to the trap of postmodern sentiment? But in spite of the issues it raises, for example, its lack of praxis, we cannot deny the importance of discussing Qoheleth's proposal in depth.

Before closing I would like to reflect briefly on the relationship between wisdom literature and apocalyptic literature. They both deal with similar situations, although there is a great difference between them: in the apocalyptic literature, the horizons remain open.

Qoheleth wrote in between the messianic promises of Isaiah, which had disappointed many Jews when they returned from exile with Esdras and Nehemiah, and apocalypticism, which emerged during Qoheleth's time or a little later. A later appearance would explain the difference between the apocalyptic vision and that of Qoheleth; Palestine fell into the power of the Seleucids and the repression was aggravated for several reasons, including the exaggerated taxation and the cultural imposition which led to the Maccabean rebellion.

If apocalypticism emerged at the same time as Qoheleth, the social position of people may explain why some were able to build a utopia and others not.

Qoheleth's book raises the suspicion that given a certain level of general economic stability, an honest person with a certain position of social privilege may suffer feelings of impotence and be unable to postulate new horizons, if the person (1) is able to satisfy basic needs, (2) is aware of the impossibility of overcoming the dominant economic and political power, and (3) has no organic links with any movement. Unable to reconstruct the awareness of a utopia contrary to the reality one is rejecting, one also rejects utopia and becomes paralyzed in the present. The past tradition that announces future promises is forgotten, because the person does not believe the promises in view of the great power of the present oppressor. Instead the person returns to the rejected present, but in reverse: magnifying the present good, because there will be nothing good in the future, or because no one knows what will come.

The apocalyptic subject who undergoes extreme suffering in the present will also reject it, like Qoheleth, but projects on the future a reality completely different from that of the present. This subject is able to reconstruct awareness and shape a utopia, in which history changes course and good overcomes evil. One is led by hope to rise above the present and resist it with dignity, by struggling against evil. Thus one can live in the midst of suffering, with trust in the near future.

Apocalypticism arose in the popular sectors and was widely accepted there. The vision of Qoheleth, as we have said, comes through the eyes of a renegade aristocrat under foreign domination. But both offer an important word about resistance to the situation.

Our present life seems different, however. The cry of suffering—"How long, O Lord?"—which is characteristic of apocalypticism, has taken precedence over the imperative, "Let us eat and drink joyfully in the midst of hard labor, for there is a time and a season for everything!"

In order to build liberating utopian horizons and live the first fruits now, with dignity, it seems important to keep both literary genres in mind. The wisdom literature is not enough to help us see the world from a structural perspective. But the apocalyptic vision, which takes in all of history at a glance, does not help us to live life from day to day, night to night, moment to moment, in the midst of enslaving labor and sorrow.

Latin American Proverbs Reflecting Qoheleth's Wisdom

ON ENSLAVING TOIL AND WORKING FOR OTHERS
(1:12-2:26)

Nadie sabe para quién trabaja.

You never know who you're working for.

Sudar la gota gorda para nada.

Working up a sweat for nothing.

Uno carga la lana y otro carga la fama.

One carries the wool, another carries the fame. (Others get the credit for what you do.)

Saberlo ganar y saberlo gastar, eso es disfrutar.

The enjoyment is in knowing how to get it and how to spend it.

Uno caza la liebre en el prado, y otro la caza en el plato.

One gets the rabbit in the field, the other gets it on a plate.

Deseando bienes y aguantando males, pasan la vida los mortales.

Mortals spend their life wishing for the good things and putting up with the bad.

La conciencia es un estorbo en el comercio.

A conscience is bad for business. (Nice guys finish last.)

La peor cazuela es guisarla y no comerla.

The worst dish is the one you cook but don't eat.

El tiempo es oro.

Time is money.

ON THE ENIGMA OF THE TIMES
AND THE INCOMPREHENSIBLE WORKS OF GOD (3:1-15)

No hay mal que cien años dure, ni persona que lo aguante.

Nothing bad lasts a hundred years, and no one lives that long anyway.

Dale lo suyo al tiempo, pero sin perder el tiento.

You can't help getting old, but you don't have to lose your touch.

Una de cal y otra de arena.

One of lime, one of sand (both needed to make cement).

Otro día será de día.

Tomorrow is another day.

La vida empieza mañana.

Tomorrow is the first day of the rest of your life.

Cuando se muera el arriero sabremos de quién son las mulas.

When the muledriver dies, we'll know whose mules they are.

No buscarle tres pies al gato.

Don't look for three feet on the cat. (Don't go looking for trouble; don't rock the boat.)

El mejor maestro, el tiempo; la mejor ciencia, la experiencia.

Time is the best teacher; experience is the best knowledge.

Dios retarda la justicia, pero no la olvida.

God holds back justice, but doesn't forget about it.

Dios aprieta pero no ahoga.

God doesn't give us more than we can take.

Tras un tiempo vendrá, y Dios dará.

God will give us what we need in good time.

Unas veces riendo y otras llorando, vamos pasando.

Sometimes we laugh, sometimes we cry.

ON THE UNHAPPINESS CAUSED BY INJUSTICE
(3:16-4:16)

Abogado, juez y doctor, cuanto más lejos, mejor.

Stay as far away as you can from lawyers, judges, and doctors.

De juez de poca conciencia no esperes justa sentencia.

You can't get a fair decision from an unfair judge.

Unos se comen la piña y a otros les duele la panza.

Some people eat the pineapple, and others get the bellyache.

Al miserable y al pobre, la pena doble.

The poor and downtrodden get twice as much sorrow.

El mundo es un mercado, serás ladrón o serás robado.

The world is a marketplace; it's either rob or get robbed.

En los ojos del patrón, verás siempre la ambición.	You can always see ambition in the boss's eyes.
Gran pena debe ser tener hambre y ver comer.	It must be hard to be hungry and see others eat.
Un alma sola, ni canta ni llora.	A lonely soul neither sings nor cries.
El avariento nunca está contento.	The greedy are never happy.
Gato dormilón, no pilla ratón.	A sleeping cat never gets the mouse.
No todos los viejos son sabios, ni todos los sabios son viejos.	Not all the old are wise, and not all the wise are old.

ON THE MYSTERY OF GOD (5:1-7)

El que mucho habla, mucho yerra.	The more one talks, the more wrong one is.
Calla, haz y con la tuya saldrás.	Stop talking, act and you'll get what you want. (Actions speak louder than words.)
El que mucho ofrece, poco da.	Those who promise much, give little.
Nunca prometas con lo que cumplir no cuentas.	Don't promise what you can't deliver.
No hacer "mucha música y nada de ópera."	Don't make "a lot of music and no opera" (opera=works).
Mucho ruido y pocas nueces.	So much rattling and so few nuts. (His bark is worse than his bite.)
Dios lo hace y él sabe por qué lo hace.	God knows what God is doing.
Habla siempre que debas, y calla siempre que puedas.	Speak whenever you have to, be quiet whenever you can. (Measure twice, cut once.)
Matrimonio y mortaja del cielo baja.	Marriages and shrouds are made in heaven.

ON THE UNHAPPINESS CAUSED BY RICHES
(5:8-20)

El que mucho abarca, poco aprieta.	Those who take on a lot, don't do much. (Don't bite off more than you can chew.)
La codicia rompe el saco.	Greed breaks open the sack. (The greedy end up with nothing.)
La rana queriendo ser vaca, reventó.	The frog puffed up until it burst, trying to be a cow.
Entre más alto más dura la caída.	The higher they are, the harder they fall.
Desnudo nací, desnudo me muero, ni gano ni pierdo.	I was born naked, I'll die naked; it's all the same to me.
Quien todo lo quiere todo lo pierde.	If you want it all, you'll lose it all.
Cuanto mayor la fortuna, tanto es menos segura.	The more you have, the harder it is to keep it.
Corazón codicioso, no tiene reposo.	A greedy heart never rests.
De la noche a la mañana pierde la oveja su lana.	It doesn't take long to shear a sheep.
La vida es corta y pasarla alegre es lo que importa.	Life is short; enjoying it is what matters.
Por mucho que uno se afane siempre hay quien le gane.	No matter how hard you try, someone can always surpass you.

ON THE UNHAPPINESS OF NOT ENJOYING LIFE
(6:1-12)

Dichas y quebrantos nos vienen de lo alto.	Happiness and tears come from on high.
Nadie se muere la víspera.	No one ever dies the night before. (In spite of the circumstances, you can keep on going.)
Todo buchón, muere pelón.	Fat and lazy people die bald.
Cada día un grano pon y harás un montón.	A grain every day adds up to a pile.

Con queso, pan y vino se anda mejor el camino.	Cheese, bread and wine make the journey easier.
Harto sabe quien sabe que no sabe.	Those who know that they do not know are wise.
Más vale pájaro en la mano, que cien volando.	A bird in the hand is better than a hundred on the wing.

ON KNOWING HOW TO RESIST (7:1-8:9)

No gozar para no sufrir, es la regla del buen vivir.	Don't enjoy, and you won't suffer; that is the rule of living well.
El corazón en Dios, y la mano donde se puede.	Give your heart to God, put your hand wherever you can.
La importancia de saber dónde aprieta el zapato.	You have to know where the shoe pinches.
Ser muy bueno no es tan bueno.	It's not good to be too good.
No se pueden pedir peras al olmo.	You can't get pears from an elm tree.
Tanto nadar para quedar en la orilla.	You swim so hard and don't get away from the shore. (It's hard to swim upstream.)
No por mucho madrugar amanece más temprano.	You can't make the dawn come by getting up early.
De dos bienes, el mayor; de dos males, el menor.	The greater of two goods, the lesser of two evils.
La mucha alegría y la mucha tristeza muerte acarrean.	Too much happiness and too much sadness, both bring death.
Ni tan corto que no alcance, ni tan duro que se pase.	Not so short it doesn't reach, nor so hard it goes through. (Choose the middle way.)
Pocos pelos, pero bien peinados.	Little hair, but well combed. (Do what you can with what you've got.)
Tiempo pasado, con pena recordado.	It's sad to remember the past.
Si tu vida es dulce, haz mermelada, si tu vida es adversa, pon la reserva.	When life is sweet, make marmalade; when times are hard, serve leftovers.

Más vale lo visto que lo que está por verse.	What you see is better than what you don't yet see.
Más vale bueno por conocido que malo por conocer.	The good you know is better than the evil you don't yet know.
Al que a buen árbol se arrima, buena sombra le cobija.	A good tree gives good shade.

ON THE INVERTED SOCIETY (8:10-9:3)

Hierba mala nunca muere.	Weeds never die. (Some people always turn up like a bad penny.)
Todos pagan los platos rotos.	Everyone pays for the broken dishes. (Everyone suffers when something goes wrong.)
Quien mal anda, más acaba.	Those who do wrong get more done. (Bad guys finish first.)
Buenos y tontos se confunden al pronto.	You can't tell who's good and who's dumb (naive).
Ahora al bueno le llaman tonto.	These days, good people are called dumb.
Una cosa piensa el burro y otra el que lo va montando.	The donkey has one plan, the rider another.
El agua para los bueyes y el vino para los reyes.	The oxen drink water, the kings drink wine.
Muerto el hombre más celebrado; a los diez días olvidado.	The most famous people are soon forgotten.
Dime con quién andas y te diré quién eres.	Tell me who you're with, and I'll tell you who you are. (We are known by the company we keep.)

ON THE ALTERNATIVE IN THE MIDST OF TOTAL FRUSTRATION: AFFIRMING REAL, EVERYDAY LIFE (9:4-9:12)

Beber y comer, buen pasatiempo es.	Drinking and eating is a good way to pass the time.

Más vale tierra en cuerpo que cuerpo en tierra.	It's better to have dirt on your body than your body in the dirt. (Better to get dirty than be killed.)
Al mejor cazador se le escapa la liebre.	The best hunter loses the rabbit. (Even experts make mistakes.)
Al mal tiempo, buen paraguas.	For bad times (or weather), a good umbrella. (Keep your parachute well mended.)
La alegría rejuvenece, la tristeza envejece.	Happiness keeps you young, sadness makes you old. (Frowning causes more wrinkles than smiling.)
Una ahora de alegría compensa diez malos días.	One hour of happiness makes up for ten bad days.

ON WISDOM IN TIMES OF "SAVE YOUR OWN SKIN" (9:13-11:6)

Hay alegrías sosas y tristezas sabrosas.	Happiness is sometimes flavorless, sadness is sometimes delicious.
Una fruta podrida echa a perder a las demás.	One rotten apple spoils the whole barrel.
Por la víspera se saca el día.	The day comes from the night before. (What we do now will make a difference tomorrow.)
Donde manda capitán no gobierna marinero.	When the captain is in charge, the sailors don't give orders.
Por la boca muere el pez.	A fish dies by its mouth. (What you say can get you in trouble.)
El que madruga come pechuga.	Those who get up early eat the chicken breast. (The early bird gets the worm.)
No hay que repartirse el cuero antes de matar la vaca.	Don't divide up the leather until you've killed the cow. (Don't count your chickens until they hatch.)
Hay que saber hasta donde estira la reata.	Don't throw the lariat until you know how long it is.

El que nació pa' tamal, del cielo le caen las hojas.	Those who are born to be tamales think the leaves fall from heaven. (Once a fool, always a fool.)
El que nace para buey, del cielo le cae la yunta.	Those who are born to be oxen, think the yoke comes down from heaven. (Once a fool, always a fool.)
El viajero se conoce por la maleta.	Travelers are known by their baggage.
La mona, aunque se vista de seda, mona se queda.	A monkey dressed in silk is still a monkey. (You can't make a silk purse out of a sow's ear. You can't take the country out of the boy.)
Muchacho barrigón ni que lo fajen chiquito.	A fat kid is still fat, even with a tight belt.
Camarón que se duerme, se lo lleva la corriente.	Sleeping shrimp get carried away by the current. (Watch what's happening around you.)
Cuando empieza a patear la mula hay que jinetearla.	When the mule starts to kick, you have to break it in. (Stay in control.)
Maña y saber para todo es menester.	Skill and knowledge are always needed.
Quien no se arriesga no gana.	Nothing ventured, nothing gained.
Estás más atravesado que el día miércoles.	You look more messed up than a Wednesday (sounds like *mierda*, shit). (You look like death warmed over.)

ON ENJOYING LIFE, BEFORE DEATH COMES
(11:7-12:7)

La vida es corta y pasarla alegre es lo que importa.	Life is short; enjoying it is what matters.
De esta vida sacarás, lo que disfrutes, nada más.	All you get out of life is what you enjoy.

El muerto al hoyo y el vivo al bollo.	The dead go in the hole, the living (also means astute or savvy) live it up. (Bury the dead; life goes on.)
El muerto al pozo y el vivo al gozo.	The dead go in the well, the living go on enjoying (approximately the same meaning as the preceding).
El día para el trabajo y la noche para descanso.	Day is for working, night is for resting.
Vivirás dulce si reprendes tu ira.	Life will be sweet if you control your anger.
A la muerte ni temerla ni buscarla; esperarla.	Don't be afraid of death, don't seek it out, just be ready for it.

NOTES

Preface

1. Biblical scholars acknowledge the difficulty of finding an internal structure in the text. Few have tried to decipher it, and I find their proposals unconvincing. The most interesting proposals are from Irene Stephanus ("Eclesiastés o Qohélet y una propuesta de hermenéutica para la ciudad a partir del rock nacional" [a thesis for the licentiate at the Facultad de Teología in Buenos Aires, 1991]); and from Norbert Lohfink (*Kohelet* [Würzburg: Echter Verlag, 1980], p. 10). I have divided the text according to the content and my proposal for reading it.

2. Most of this introduction appeared in "La razón utópica de Qohélet," *Pasos* (DEI), no. 52 (March-April 1994): 9-23.

Introduction

1. Franz Hinkelammert, "La lógica de la exclusión del mercado capitalista mundial y el proyecto de liberación," in *América Latina: Resistir por la vida* (San José: REDLA-CPID, 1994).

2. This is the opinion of most scholars. Some date it earlier, in the Persian Empire, and others later, in the second century B.C.E. (see José Vílchez Lindez, *Eclesiastés o Qohélet* [Estella: Verbo Divino, 1994], pp. 80-83). Although my reading places it in the second half of the third century, a date in the Persian period would not change it significantly. This affirmation agrees with the analysis of the socioeconomic and political context in a recent commentary by Choon-Leong Seow (*Ecclesiastes,* Anchor Bible [New York: Doubleday, 1997], pp. 21-36).

3. Gianfranco Ravasi, *Qohélet* (Bogotá: Paulinas, 1991), p. 40.

4. The work ends at 12:8; vv. 9-14 are later additions by another hand.

5. The connotations of these words are not entirely satisfactory. "Rubbish" implies dirtiness, but the term *hebel* does not. I think of "rubbish" as a synonym for today's common meaning of "shit."

Although this word originally meant something dirty in our culture, most of its uses today have a different connotation. "Shit!" is a common expression of uncontrolled frustration in almost every language. However there are some places in this book—a few—where *hebel* is used differently. When it refers to the stage of youth, it means "ephemeral."

6. Ravasi, op. cit., pp. 9ff.

7. The term is used often in the Book of Qoheleth; of fifty-seven occurrences in the Hebrew Bible, thirty-five are in Qoheleth. The same is true of *hebel:* of seventy-three occurrences in the Hebrew Bible, forty-one are in Qoheleth (E. Jenni-C. Westermann, *Diccionario teológico manual del Antiguo Testamento* [Madrid: Cristiandad, 1978], vol. 1, pp. 423, 660).

8. The Reina Valera translation in Spanish, following the Vulgate, renders *ri'ut ruah* ("trapping the wind") as "affliction of the spirit," thus expressing the anguish of the subject.

9. Longevity and many children, in the Hebrew tradition, were seen as evidence of God's blessing.

10. This is 5:7 in the Hebrew. The enumeration of the text in the Valera version (also in the New Revised Standard Version) changes in chapter 5.

11. This was the perception in Hellenism during that time with *heimarmenē*, the power that determines human life. See Helmut Koester, *Introducción al Nuevo Testamento: Historia, cultura y religión de la época helenística e historia y literatura del cristianismo primitivo* (Salamanca: Sígueme, 1988), pp. 210ff.

12. See M. Rostovtzeff, *Histoire Economique et Sociale du Monde Hellénistique* (Paris: Editions Robert Laffont, S.A., 1989), pp. 185ff.

13. Alexander conquered Palestine in 333-332 B.C.E. Ptolemy I and Seleucus I were fighting for power. Ptolemy ended up with Egypt; Seleucus got western Syria and the East, through Iran. Both wanted Palestine and Phoenicia; the Ptolemies won the battle and ruled Palestine for nearly a century. During that time the Seleucids repeatedly tried and failed to dislodge the Ptolemies. The Seleucid Antiochus III finally succeeded at the end of the century, in the year 200 B.C.E.

14. Martin Hengel, *Judaism and Hellenism* (Philadelphia: Fortress Press, 1974), pp. 6-57; Rostovtzeff, op. cit., pp. 170-301, 728-950; and *Greece* (New York: Oxford University Press, 1963), pp. 258-300; Koester, op. cit., pp. 73-345; Stephan deJong, "¡Quítate de mi sol! Eclesiastés y la tecnocracia helenística," *RIBLA* (Costa Rica, DEI), no. 11 (1992): 75-85.

15. There was extensive agricultural development with irrigation, new plants, improved nutrients, and the invention of the chain pump

for use in the marshlands. One Philadelphia farm was considered an agricultural experiment station; in Palestine there were artificial terraces, reservoirs, and canals (Hengel, op. cit., p. 44).

16. This was the age of Archimedes, Euclid, Aristarchus of Samos, Apollonius of Perga, and others.

17. Hengel, op. cit., p. 13.

18. Claude Orrieux, *Les papyrus de Zenon: L'horizon d'un grec en Egypte au IIIe siècle avant J.C.* (Paris: Macula, 1983).

19. Ibid., p. 19.

20. Rostovtzeff, *Histoire Economique,* op. cit., pp. 267-71, 781.

21. Hengel quotes this expression by W. W. Tarn.

22. Frederic Madden, *History of Jewish Coinage and of Money in the Old and New Testament* (San Diego: Calif.: Pegasus Pub. Co., 1967), p. 22.

23. Hengel, op. cit., p. 44.

24. Ibid., p. 17.

25. Rostovtzeff, *Greece,* op. cit., p. 274.

26. Ibid., p. 272.

27. Robert Michaud, *Qohélet y el helenismo* (Estella: Ed. Verbo Divino, 1988), p. 129.

28. Hengel, op. cit., p. 48.

29. Ibid., p. 39.

30. Anna Maria Rizzante and Sandro Gallazzi, "La prueba de los ojos, la prueba de la casa, la prueba del sepulcro: Una clave de lectura del libro de Qohélet," *RIBLA,* no. 14 (1993): 64ff.

31. DeJong, op. cit., p. 82.

32. Ravasi, op. cit., p. 14; Aarre Lauha, *Kohelet,* Biblischer Kommentar Altes Testament (Neukirchen-Vluyn: Neukirchener Verlag, 1978), p. 1; deJong, op. cit., pp. 81-83.

33. However, one should be cautious about identifying him with Solomon, because he presents himself as king in a critical way.

34. Hengel, op. cit., p. 48.

35. Michaud, op. cit., pp. 126-31.

36. His thinking may have been influenced by the Greek philosophy of the Cynics or the Epicureans, who were his contemporaries, but I believe he is reinterpreting these concepts from his Jewish viewpoint.

37. Irene Stephanus, "Eclesiastés o Qohélet y una propuesta de hermenéutica para la ciudad a partir del rock nacional" (thesis for the licentiate at the Facultad de Teología in Buenos Aires, 1991), pp. 37, 104, 106.

38. For this analysis we shall use some basic categories of Franz Hinkelammert, mostly from his book *Crítica a la razón utópica* (San José: DEI, 1984), and in "El cautiverio de la utopía: Las utopías con-

servadoras del capitalismo actual, el neoliberalismo y la dialéctica de las alternativas," *Pasos,* no. 50 (November-December, 1993): 1-14.

39. Hans Walter Wolff, *Antropología del Antiguo Testamento* (Salamanca: Sígueme, 1975), pp. 71-82.

40. It is interesting that during the same time, there was a struggle in Alexandria between the middle academy and the stoa over the knowledge of truth. The Platonist Academics preferred to abstain from judgment, because in their view, every argument can be answered with another; the Stoics, like the Epicureans, affirmed that one can arrive at the truth through ideas gained from experience, through scientific perception. See Koester, op. cit., p. 197.

41. Hinkelammert, "El cautiverio de la utopía," op. cit., p. 13.

42. The Hebrew word ʿet (time) corresponds to the Greek *kairos,* which refers to the opportune, ripe time. In the New Testament it corresponds to the coming of the era of Jesus Christ.

43. *Tob* means happiness, goodness, beauty.

44. See 2:24-26; 3:12-13; 3:22; 5:17-19; 8:15; and 9:7-10. In 11:9-10 he also advises youth to rejoice and be happy in their youth.

45. Hinkelammert describes utopia as the construction of impossible worlds (*Crítica a la razón utópica*). Politics would be the art of the possible, guided by a vision of the impossible.

46. In the words of Rizzante and Gallazzi, this seems to be a micropsalm for everyday life (op. cit., p. 82).

47. Marvin Pope, *Song of Songs,* Anchor Bible (New York: Doubleday, 1977), p. 210ff.

48. These changes do not appear in orderly fashion in the text, and they need not, because this is a struggle in his own consciousness.

49. Jenni-Westermann, op. cit., p. 1066.

50. Franz Mussner, *Tratado sobre los judíos* (Salamanca: Sígueme, 1983), p. 98.

51. I am using the Reina Valera translation in Spanish, with slight changes at some points in consideration of the original Hebrew and contemporary inclusive language.

The Prologues

1. See Amos 1:1; Jeremiah 1:1; Nehemiah 1:1. Gianfranco Ravasi, *Qohelet* (Bogotá: Paulinas, 1991), p. 51. Scholars say that this verse is an introduction added by the author of the epilogue in 12:9-10.

2. Graham Ogden considers "one who argues" a more appropriate translation, as in Nehemiah 5:7 (*Qoheleth* [Sheffield: JSOT Press, 1987], p. 27). Alphonse Maillot points out a resemblance between the roots qhl and qll, which means "to criticize or contest" (*Qohélet ou*

L'Ecclesiaste ou la constatation [Paris: Les Bergers et le Mages, 1987], p. ix).

3. On the complexity of the word see José Vílchez Lindez, *Eclesiastés o Qohélet* (Estella: Verbo Divino, 1994), pp. 425-31; Ravasi, op. cit., p. 11f.

4. The apposition "son of Jerusalem" refers to the preacher, not to David. Aarre Lauha, *Kohelet*, Biblischer Kommentar Altes Testament (Neukirchen-Vluyn: Neukirchener Verlag, 1978), p. 2. The commentators note that the construction of the phrase "king in Jerusalem" is unusual; normally it is either king of Judah or of Israel.

5. R. N. Whybray affirms that 1:2 and 12:8 are a synthesis of Qoheleth's thinking, interpreted by another editor. Qoheleth's own words would then begin in 1:4. For Qoheleth, says Whybray, not everything is vanity (cf. 3:11), but only what he identifies in concrete situations (*Ecclesiastes*, New Century Bible Commentary [London: Wm. B. Eerdmans, 1989], p. 35ff.).

6. Other biblical examples include the Song of Songs, which would mean the most beautiful song, or the king of kings, the absolute king.

7. Michael V. Fox, *Qohelet and His Contradictions* (Sheffield: Almond Press, 1989), pp. 29-37.

8. E. Jenni-C. Westermann, *Diccionario teológico manual del Antiguo Testamento* (Madrid: Cristiandad, 1978), vol. 1, p. 661.

9. According to Ogden (op. cit., p. 14) the word has nothing to do with vanity or "meaninglessness," but rather describes the enigmatic, the ironic dimension of human life.

10. According to R. Pautrel (*L'Ecclésiaste* [Paris: Cerf, 1953]), the word conveys no substantive value but simply expresses a sense of disillusionment.

11. Fox, op. cit., p. 33. André Barucq (*Eclesiastés, Qoheleth: Texto y comentario* [Madrid: Ed. Fax, 1971]) also prefers the term absurd.

Section I

1. Graham Ogden, *Qoheleth* (Sheffield: JSOT Press, 1987), p. 28.

2. The words *motar* (superiority) (3:19) and *yoter* (advantage, abundance) also come from *ytr*.

3. Choon-Leong Seow, *Ecclesiastes*, Anchor Bible (New York: Doubleday, 1997), p. 103.

4. In chapter 5 there is a different enumeration in the Hebrew and the Valera (also NRSV) translation.

5. It appears with significant frequency (out of fifty-seven appearances in the Hebrew Bible, thirty-five are in the Book of Qoheleth).

See E. Jenni-C. Westermann, *Diccionario teológico manual del Antiguo Testamento* (Madrid: Cristiandad, 1978), vol. 1, p. 423.

6. Ibid., p. 426.

7. This is especially true when it appears together with the verb. See R. N. Whybray, *Ecclesiastes,* New Century Bible Commentary (London: Wm. B. Eerdmans, 1989), p. 37.

8. Gianfranco Ravasi, *Qoheleth* (Bogotá: Paulinas, 1991), p. 56; Aarre Lauha, *Kohelet,* Biblischer Kommentar Altes Testament (Neukirchen-Vluyn: Neukirchener Verlag, 1978), p. 33.

9. Anna Maria Rizzante and Sandro Gallazzi, "La prueba de los ojos, la prueba de la casa, la prueba del sepulcro: Una clave de lectura del libro de Qohélet," *RIBLA,* no. 14 (1993): 63.

10. Ravasi, op. cit., p. 57.

11. James L. Crenshaw, *Ecclesiastes: A Commentary* (London: SCM Press, 1988), p. 62.

12. The same principle underlies the movement of the generations in v. 4a, and the sun in vv. 5-7. See Ogden, op. cit., p. 30; Vittoria D'Alario, *Il Libro del Qoheleth: Struttura letteraria e retorica* (Bologna: Centro Editoriale Dehoniano, 1992), p. 78.

13. Ogden, op. cit., p. 32.

14. Segismundo, the character in *La vida es sueño* by Calderón de la Barca, has a line that describes very well the meaning of this text: "My eyes must have dropsy, for when to drink is death, they drink more; thus, seeing that to see means death to me, I am dying because I see." Dropsy is a pathological thirst (*La vida es sueño* [San Salvador: Clásicos Roxil, 1985], p. 30).

15. Thus the French *Traduction Œcuménique de la Bible,* an ecumenical translation (Paris: Cerf, 1988).

16. In all the stories, when the mythological character Wannadi thinks or dreams of food, animals, life, or death, what he thinks appears or happens. See Marc de Civrieux, *Watunna, mitología makiritare* (Caracas: Monte Avila editores, 1970).

17. Crenshaw, op. cit., p. 66.

18. D'Alario, op. cit., p. 79.

19. Ravasi, op. cit., p. 61.

20. In *Unica mirando al mar* (San José: Farben Grupo Editorial Norma, 1994), p. 11.

21. Ibid., pp. 85 ff.

22. Whybray, op. cit., p. 48; Seow, op. cit., p. 120.

23. Alphonse Maillot suggests that Qoheleth did not have in mind the royal and humble wisdom (*hokmah*) of Israelite tradition, but

rather the wisdom (*sophia*) of his time, which believed that if ideas are in order the world will order itself (*Qohélet ou L'Ecclesiaste ou la constatation* [Paris: Les Bergers et le Mages, 1987], pp. 10f.).

24. *Tur,* "to investigate," is the word addressed to the spies sent out by Joshua.

25. This is one literal translation of *ᶜinyan raᶜ*. There is nothing to be gained from it.

26. Ogden, op. cit., p. 35.

27. Michael V. Fox, *Qohelet and His Contradictions* (Sheffield, The Almond Press, 1989), pp. 48-51.

28. Crenshaw, op. cit., p. 76.

29. Qoheleth uses *heleq* (portion) repeatedly in the book. This term was used in assigning a parcel of land or an inheritance; here it is used figuratively (Seow, op. cit., p. 151). Rizzante and Gallazzi suggest that this reflects "the memory of a time when the criterion was distribution according to needs (Numbers 33:53f.)." They see it as a criticism of the slave-based latifundio system of the Greeks. A portion for everyone, as opposed to the profit of a few, is good for security (Rizzante and Gallazzi, op. cit., p. 79).

30. Whybray, op. cit., p. 54.

31. Madness and folly are used here as a hendiadys, a rhetorical figure meaning madness or idiocy without purpose.

32. The second part of v. 12 does not fit the context very well; moreover, it appears in the third person rather than the first person with which the section begins. Lauha (op. cit., p. 56) considers it a gloss.

33. Whybray, op. cit., p. 60.

34. M. Rostovtzeff, *Histoire Economique et Sociale du Monde Hellénistique* (Paris: Editions Robert Laffont, S.A., 1989), p. 192.

35. Martin Hengel, *Judaism and Hellenism* (Philadelphia: Fortress Press, 1974), p. 39.

36. See 2:24-26; 3:12-13; 3:22; 5:17-19; 8:15; and 9:7-16; in 11:9-10 he also advises young people to rejoice and be cheerful in their youth.

37. The translation is questionable. In the Hebrew some manuscripts have "apart from me"; others have "apart from him." Some versions translate it with God as the subject; that is, apart from God who gives life and enjoyment.

38. Here the Hebrew word *hoteᵓ* does not have a religious connotation. It refers to one who constantly commits errors, misses the target, or goes astray (Crenshaw, op. cit., p. 90). To Seow (op. cit., p. 141) it means a "loser"; the antonym would be one who is astute or able.

Section II

1. I agree with the meaning that John R. Wilch assigns to the concept of ʿet in Qoheleth, though not with his overall interpretation of the text. See John R. Wilch, *Time and Event: An Exegetical Study of the Use of* et *in the Old Testament in Comparison to Other Temporal Expressions in Clarification of the Concept of Time* (Leiden: E. J. Brill, 1969).

2. This poetic style was common in the Hebrew Bible and generally in the literature of the Near East. Qoheleth may have borrowed it from the literature to present his argument, although he interprets it from his own viewpoint. See R. N. Whybray, *Ecclesiastes,* New Century Bible Commentary (London: Wm. B. Eerdmans, 1989), p. 67.

3. James L. Crenshaw, *Ecclesiastes: A Commentary* (London: SCM Press, 1988), p. 92.

4. Aarre Lauha, *Kohelet,* Biblischer Kommentar Altes Testament (Neukirchen-Vluyn: Neukirchener Verlag, 1978), p. 64. According to Gianfranco Ravasi, *zman* means a moment of duration, a period, the chronological aspect of time. The term ʿet refers more to an opportunity, a propitious time. See Gianfranco Ravasi, *Qohelet* (Bogotá: Paulinas, 1991), p. 103.

5. Graham Ogden, *Qoheleth* (Sheffield: JSOT Press, 1987), p. 52.

6. Wilch, op. cit., p. 102.

7. Some scholars suggest that to pluck up what is planted means to harvest; but the antithetical placement seems to indicate a negative meaning.

8. Ogden, op. cit., p. 53.

9. Ibid.

10. José Vílchez Lindez, *Eclesiastés o Qohélet* (Estella: Verbo Divino, 1994), p. 231; Ravasi, op. cit., p. 105.

11. For a complete chiastic analysis, see Vittoria D'Alario, *Il Libro del Qohelet: Struttura letteraria e retorica* (Bologna: Centro Editoriale Dehoniano, 1992), pp. 101-4.

12. Alphonse Maillot, *Qohélet ou L'Ecclesiaste ou la constatation* (Paris: Les Bergers et le Mages, 1987), p. 34.

13. *De cuentos de angustias y paisajes.* Quoted in Fernando Contreras Castro, *Unica mirando al mar* (San José: Farben Grupo Editorial Norma, 1994), p. 10.

14. Here the Hebrew term is not ʿamal (enslaving toil), but ʿinyan (occupation).

15. Others have amended ʿolam in order to read it as ignorance. See Whybray, op. cit., p. 74.

16. Cf. Deuteronomy 4:2; it is also used in Matthew 13:1.

17. Ravasi, op. cit., p. 109.

18. Whybray, op. cit., p. 76.

19. This may refer to the enjoyment of God's gifts, of what God does. Ogden, op. cit., p. 58.

20. Robert Michaud, *Qohélet y el helenismo* (Estella: Verbo Divino, 1988), p. 194.

21. I do not agree with those who consider this the insertion of a pious editor.

22. Cf. Psalms 11:5-7; 58:12; 89:15; 97:12; etc.

23. The syntax of this verse is rather difficult; I interpret it in line with the context set by chapter 3.

24. "Sons of Adam" simply means human beings. Perhaps the word ʾ*adam* is retained here as a reference to the legacy of death.

25. *Hebel* in 3:19 has the meaning of "ephemeral," "transitory."

26. M. Rostovtzeff, *Histoire Economique et Sociale du Monde Hellénistique* (Paris: Editions Robert Laffont, S.A., 1989), pp. 781-83; Stephan deJong, "¡Quítate de mi sol! Eclesiastés y la tecnocracia helenística," *RIBLA* (Costa Rica, DEI), no. 11 (1992): 80.

27. With respect to immortality, Choon-Leong Seow (*Ecclesiastes*, Anchor Bible [New York: Doubleday, 1997], p. 175) suggests that in equating humans with beasts, Qoheleth is referring not to their quality of life but to the mortality they share.

28. Cf. Psalm 104:29; Job 34:15.

29. The Hebrew text uses the same word (*ruah*) for "breath" in v. 19 and "spirit" in v. 21. This suggests that in Hebrew thought there is not much difference between the two translations of *ruah*.

30. Crenshaw, op. cit., p. 105.

31. For the meaning of *heleq*, see the note on 2:10 in the preceding section.

32. Ogden, op. cit., p. 65f.

33. Ravasi, op. cit., p. 121, who cites D. Lys.

34. Ibid., p. 121.

35. Michaud, op. cit., p. 198. Cf. Nehemiah 5:2, two centuries earlier.

36. Whybray, op. cit., p. 83.

37. Michaud, op. cit., p. 199.

38. Ibid., p. 200.

39. Cf. Proverbs 6:6, 9; 11:6; 20:4; 21:25; 22:13; 24:30, etc.

40. Cf. Jeremiah 19:9; Ezekiel 39:18; Micah 3:3.

41. Seow, op. cit., p. 187.

42. Ravasi, op. cit., p. 126.

43. Lauha (op. cit., p. 89) interprets "the second" (*shny*) as a companion. Vílchez agrees (op. cit., p. 265).

44. The reference is not to a man and woman lying together. It was an oriental custom, especially among bedouins and farmers, to withstand the intense nighttime cold by sleeping side-by-side for warmth (cf. Ruth 3; Ravasi, op. cit., p. 129; Crenshaw, op. cit., p. 111; Lauha, op. cit., p. 190; Seow, op. cit., p. 189; cf. 1 Kings 1:1-2; 2 Kings 32-34).

45. This proverb speaks of three as the ideal; the preceding verses speak of two. There seems to be a discontinuity between the two verses. The ascending numerical order may explain it: v. 8 speaks of one, vv. 9-12a of two, and v. 12b of three people. Moreover, if two are better than one, three are better yet. In any case, the verses are thematically linked to make the point that in unity there is strength.

46. Crenshaw, op. cit., p. 112.

47. According to Ogden (op. cit., p. 72), to be in power may mean not only to rule but also to be an advisor to the ruler.

48. Ibid., p. 72.

49. Michaud, op. cit., p. 202.

50. Whybray, op. cit., p. 89.

51. Vílchez, op. cit., p. 268.

52. The Hebrew text has a different enumeration of the verses in chapter 5. 5:1 is numbered as 4:17, 5:2 as 5:1, and so on. The Hebrew enumeration is shown in square brackets.

53. The same idea is present on a Hurrite-Canaanite tablet in the *Instruction of Merikare,* from the year 2000 B.C.E. (Ravasi, op. cit., p. 137).

54. Ogden, op. cit., p. 76.

55. Vílchez, op. cit., p. 273.

56. Seow, op. cit., p. 194.

57. This idea is typical of the wisdom style. Cf. Proverbs 10:9; also other wisdom sources such as the *Instruction of Ani,* from Egypt.

58. Whybray, op. cit., p. 94.

59. The meaning of the first part of the saying is unclear. Some believe he is speaking of the visions or ecstasy of believers in the temple, but this is not clear in Qoheleth's context.

60. Ravasi, op. cit., p. 138.

61. Whybray, op. cit., p. 94.

62. Rostovtzeff, op. cit., p. 770.

63. Kathleen A. Farmer, *Proverbs & Ecclesiastes: Who Knows What Is Good* (Grand Rapids: Wm. B. Eerdmans, 1991), p. 168.

64. Ogden, op. cit., p. 80.

65. Whybray, op. cit., p. 97.

66. Crenshaw, op. cit., p. 118.

67. Ravasi, op. cit., p. 147.

68. Ibid., p. 148.

69. The Hebrew word for silver is used here, since silver coins were the most common form of money.

70. Ross Kinsler and Gloria Kinsler, *The Biblical Jubilee and the Struggle for Life* (Maryknoll, New York: Orbis Books, 1999).

71. Whybray, op. cit., p. 100.

72. Ogden, op. cit., p. 84.

73. The term appears twice, in vv. 13 and 16.

74. This may be a variant of the expression, "chasing the wind."

75. Ravasi, op. cit., p. 151.

76. The TOB version renders the mood of the accumulator as "afflicted, depressed, and irritated."

77. Here again Qoheleth uses the word *ḥôly,* as in 5:13, 16, and 17 [Heb. vv. 12, 15, and 16].

78. *Rabah*—"great," rather than heavy or onerous—means broad and extensive (Ogden, op. cit., p. 90).

79. These are the same things attributed to Solomon in 2 Chronicles 1:11-12. But unlike the Solomon in Qoheleth 2:10, these rich cannot enjoy their goods.

80. The literal meaning of *nefesh,* which is often translated as "soul" or "life," is "throat." Here the emphasis is on the material aspect.

81. The literal meaning of *ʾakal* is "to eat or consume." The figure is very concrete; it means using one's goods for oneself.

82. E. Jenni-C. Westermann, *Diccionario teológico manual del Antiguo Testamento* (Madrid: Cristiandad, 1978), vol. 1, p. 98.

83. Michaud, op. cit., p. 214.

84. Since it is not clear what Qoheleth means by this, there have been attempts to emend it. For instance, Robert Gordis suggests changing the negative formulation to affirmative: "Even if it had a (good) funeral" (quoted by Ogden, op. cit., p. 92).

85. Whybray, op. cit., p. 105; cf. 2 Kings 9:33-37; Jeremiah 22:18-19.

86. Ogden, op. cit., p. 92.

87. Lauha, op. cit., p. 114.

88. "Mouth" may refer to *sheol,* the place of the dead. In some literature it is personified as insatiably devouring men and women (Proverbs 27:20; 30:16; Isaiah 5:14; Habakkuk 2:5) (Crenshaw, op. cit., p. 128). This interpretation is not inconsistent with Qoheleth's description of death as an inevitable destiny for all. But if the verse is drawn from an aphorism, the literal meaning of "mouth" is preferable.

89. The Hebrew term is *nefesh.* Its original meaning is throat (see

n. 80 above), but it can be translated as "desire," or "soul." In Proverbs 16:26 it is translated as "mouth" and "appetite."

90. Amendments have been made to this verse, without basis in the ancient versions. Poor (ʿany) has been interpreted as "humble" or "pious" in v. 8b, in order to establish a parallel with the wise in v. 8a.

91. Qoheleth draws a connection between the poor and the wise in 4:13 and 9:15.

92. Seow, op. cit., p. 217.

93. The meaning in Hebrew has judicial connotations, as in the book of Job.

94. All the discourses of Job and his friends are litigious. Job demands accountability from God for the injustice committed against the innocent; his friends play the part of lawyers, defending God and blaming Job.

Section III

1. This is an onomatopoeic wordplay in the Hebrew.

2. According to Kathleen A. Farmer, Qoheleth is not recommending the contemplation of death in a morbid sense, but to persuade his readers that life is too short to waste. *Proverbs & Ecclesiastes: Who Knows What Is Good* (Grand Rapids: Wm. B. Eerdmans, 1991), p. 175.

3. Alphonse Maillot, *Qohélet ou L'Ecclesiaste ou la constatation* (Paris: Les Bergers et le Mages, 1987), p. 93.

4. "In my vain life" means during his short life.

5. M. Rostovtzeff, *Histoire Economique et Sociale du Monde Hellénistique* (Paris: Editions Robert Laffont, S.A., 1989), p. 785.

6. I agree with Seow that ʿebed does not necessarily mean a slave. A high official can be an ʿebed to another official. Thus the word in this context means a subordinate. See Choon-Leong Seow, *Ecclesiastes,* Anchor Bible (New York: Doubleday, 1997), p. 258.

7. James L. Crenshaw, *Ecclesiastes: A Commentary* (London: SCM Press, 1988), p. 143.

8. The use of *rehoqah* and ʿamoq in 7:23-24 emphasizes the distance and the depth of wisdom. Spatial categories also appear in 1:13 (Crenshaw, op. cit., p. 145).

9. Wisdom and reason (*hokmah* and *heshbon*) form a rhetorical hendiadys and constitute the sum total of knowledge (Crenshaw, op. cit., p. 145).

10. R. N. Whybray, *Ecclesiastes,* New Century Bible Commentary (London: Wm.B. Eerdmans, 1989), p. 124.

11. The word *mar* also means "strong." There was a saying that woman was stronger than death. The Song of Songs says that love is as strong as death. 1 Samuel 15:32 speaks of the bitterness of death. Here, in Ecclesiastes 7:26, Qoheleth is probably thinking about bitterness rather than strength.

12. Curiously, this is the only place where the verb accompanying the name Qoheleth appears in a feminine form. Most commentators consider it an error.

13. He uses the generic word *ʾadam*. Perhaps because of its antithetical placement with *ʾishah* (woman), he is specifically referring to a male.

14. The Hebrew term *hishbonot* (NRSV: schemes) means machinations or intrigues. It only appears here and in 2 Chronicles 26:15, where it refers to preparations for war.

15. Irene Stephanus, "Eclesiastés o Qohéleth y una propuesta de heremenéutica para la ciudad a partir del rock nacional" (thesis for the licentiate at the Facultad de Teología, Buenos Aires, 1991), p. 106f.

16. Aarre Lauha, *Kohelet,* Biblischer Kommentar Altes Testament (Neukirchen-Vluyn: Neikirchener Verlag, 1978), p. 148.

17. Ibid.

18. According to Gianfranco Ravasi (*Qohélet* [Bogotá: Paulinas, 1991], p. 185), to leave the king's presence in haste may be a violation of court etiquette, an official break, or an omission of official acts.

19. Lauha, op. cit., p. 148.

20. Note that here Qoheleth introduces a new term, "judgment," to go with the word "time." It may mean an exact time or a time and a method (Ravasi, op. cit., p. 186).

21. Vittoria D'Alario, *Il Libro del Qohelet: Struttura letteraria e retorica* (Bologna: Centro Editoriale Dehoniano, 1992), p. 151.

22. *Ruah* can be translated as "wind" or "spirit." If it is translated as "spirit," Qoheleth is referring to the human inability to hold on to life. That would make it parallel with the following clause.

23. The last part of this verse is strange. It may refer to the perverse tyranny of the king, who cannot escape death. Others amend "wickedness" to "riches." It can then be applied to either the king or the rich. Their possessions will do them no good when the time of death comes.

24. For instance, the Reina Valera (Spanish) version chooses to identify "the holy place" with the righteous ones: "but those who frequented the holy place were later forgotten in the city where they had acted with righteousness."

25. The use of the plural means that it occurs frequently (Graham Ogden, *Qoheleth* [Sheffield: JSOT Press, 1987], p. 135).

26. Cf. Job 21:32-33.

27. Ravasi, op. cit., p. 188.

28. Others take the holy place to mean the cemetery; if so it would be the burial ceremony. In any case, it is a place related to religious matters.

29. Ogden, op. cit., p. 135.

30. Maillot, op. cit., p. 124.

31. Whybray, op. cit., p. 136.

32. Other translations read the text according to Qoheleth's critique of the doctrine of retribution from the preceding verses. In this case I prefer to interpret the texts as a positive affirmation of the received tradition. The French translation TOB does the same. *'Asher* can be translated here as "although."

33. Alternatively: they go around it (ignore the sentence).

34. Also see Proverbs 14:2, 27.

35. Cf. Job 21:7, 13.

36. Crenshaw, op. cit., p. 157.

37. On this problem, cf. 3:11; 7:13, 14, 24, 29.

38. Cf. D'Alario, op. cit., p. 154.

39. Ogden, op. cit., p. 141.

40. These are what happens under the sun. Cf. ibid., p. 141.

41. It is an act of faith, not knowledge, says Ogden (op. cit., p. 144).

42. Here righteous and wise appear to be synonyms.

43. Some commentators suggest that he is referring to passionate human feelings. Love and hate would be polar opposites, as in 3:8, covering the spectrum of feelings (Whybray, op. cit., p. 140).

44. Ravasi, op. cit., p. 197.

45. Ogden, op. cit., p. 145.

46. In this sense I have called Qoheleth a text of resistance. See also Stephanus, op. cit., pp. 37-106.

47. Some versions translate the term as "hope," but that is not exact. According to Seow, it is the confidence or certainty that something will happen.

48. There is a wordplay in Hebrew with the terms *sakar* and *zeker,* "reward" and "memory."

49. In Hebrew, the word *ratsah* means to approve and to take delight.

50. Some versions translate the word *'ishah* as "wife"; however, the definite article does not appear in the Hebrew, and there is no reason to limit it to the conjugal relationship.

51. Ogden, op. cit., p. 153.

52. Quoted by Ravasi, op. cit., p. 201. He also cites the following sentence from the Babylonian Talmud: "They are also sinners who deprive themselves of all blessings" (*Erubin* 54a).

53. Part of the poem, "La tiránica ley de la muerte," translated and presented by Angel M. Garibay K. in *La literatura de los aztecas* (Mexico, D.Fl: Ed. Joaquín Mortiz, 1964), p. 68.

54. "Error," "mistake," or "sin" is an emendation of "sinner" (*hote*'), which means missing the mark.

55. See Farmer, op. cit., p. 187.

56. Crenshaw, op. cit., p. 170.

57. According to Maillot (op. cit., p. 145), the context suggests a reference to men of importance, generally wealthy, of noble origin.

58. See Robert Michaud, *Qohelet y el helenismo* (Estella: Verbo Divino, 1988), p. 43.

59. José Vílchez Lindez, *Eclesiastés o Qohélet* (Estella: Verbo Divino, 1994), p. 376.

60. Seow, op. cit., p. 369.

61. Vílchez, op. cit., p. 378.

62. Snake charming (here, literally, mastery of the tongue) was a common custom in Egypt and Mesopotamia. See Ravasi, op. cit., p. 218.

63. See Whybray, op. cit., p. 155.

64. Ogden, op. cit., p. 176.

65. Michaud, op. cit., p. 247.

66. The whole chapter contrasts foolishness with wisdom; here it contrasts the behavior of a wise king with that of a foolish king. See Ogden, op. cit., p. 176.

67. Maillot, op. cit., pp. 151f. Crenshaw (op. cit., p. 177) draws a closer connection between v. 19 and v. 16.

68. Maillot (op. cit., p. 150) prefers to translate this word as "important men" rather than "the rich."

69. Stephanus (op. cit., p. 107) affirms that sharing is at the heart of Qoheleth's discourse. She comes to that conclusion by analyzing the somewhat complex structure that begins precisely at v. 2 (pp. 50ff.; also see "Qohélet," *RIBLA,* no. 15 [1992]: 75-85).

70. This may be a dual reference: we do not understand where the wind blows, or how bones are formed in the uterus. Or it may be a single reference, to the breath of life that gives life to the bones. Biblical commentators and translators differ on this point.

71. Ravasi, op. cit., p. 231. This is a common metaphor in the Hebrew Bible (cf. Isaiah 5:20). Qoheleth also says in 5:12 [Heb. 5:11] that the sleep of laborers is sweet.

72. Lauha, op. cit., p. 208.

73. Vílchez, op. cit., p. 396.

74. See Ogden, op. cit.; D'Alario, op. cit.; Ravasi, op. cit.; and others.

75. In Hebrew the jussive mode is more gentle than the imperative.

76. Youth and adolescence ("the dawn of life") are used here as synonyms.

77. Vílchez, op. cit., p. 398.

78. Ravasi, op. cit., p. 232. Cf. Ruth 2:14; 1 Kings 21:7.

79. D'Alario, op. cit., p. 169.

80. It appears in the plural in Hebrew. In spite of the amendments that have been made to *bor'eyka*, the best translation is still "Creator." See Seow, op. cit., p. 351.

81. Vílchez, op. cit., p. 402.

82. Several commentators have seen an allegory of old age in the description of the house. The guards and the strong men are the trembling arms and legs of the elderly; the grinding mills refer to their failing teeth; the windows are their eyes that no longer see. That interpretation of the text has lost currency in recent years.

83. The second part of the verse, which speaks of nature, has also been interpreted as a contrast with old age. The almond is the first tree that blooms in the spring; grasshoppers and caper berries appear in midsummer; while old age means only winter, with no hope of the rebirth that comes to nature. I prefer to read it as a metaphor of old age, as the harbinger of death, which follows immediately in the same verse.

84. Farmer, op. cit., p. 194.

85. The pulley was brought to Palestine in the third century B.C.E., during Qoheleth's time.

Epilogues

1. Most writers see two epilogues: vv. 9-11 and vv. 12-14. I would add 12:8 as an overall epilogue to Qoheleth's discourse, before the appendix in 12:9-14. A few other writers divide the appendix into three epilogues: vv. 9-11, v. 12, and vv. 13-14. Some others see vv. 9-14 as a single epilogue by one author.

2. José Vílchez Lindez, *Eclesiastés o Qohélet* (Estella: Verbo Divino, 1994), p. 415.

3. Ibid., p. 417.

4. Robert Michaud, *Qohélet y el helenismo* (Estella: Verbo Divino, 1988), p. 261.

5. R. N. Whybray, *Ecclesiastes,* New Century Bible Commentary (London: Wm. B. Eerdmans, 1989), p. 174.